THE MOST FORBIDDEN KNOWLEDGE

151 THINGS **NO ONE** SHOULD KNOW HOW TO DO

Michael Powell
and
Matt Forbeck

Avon, Massachusetts

Published by Adams Media, a division of F+W Media, Inc.
57 Littlefield Street
Avon, MA 02322. U.S.A.
www.adamsmedia.com

ISBN 10: 1-4405-6092-7
ISBN 13: 978-1-4405-6092-7
eISBN 10: 1-4405-6093-5
eISBN 13: 978-1-4405-6093-4

Printed in the United States of America.

Contains material adapted and abridged from *Forbidden Knowledge* by Michael
Powell, copyright © 2007 by Gusto Company AS, ISBN 10: 1-59869-525-8, ISBN
13: 978-1-59869-525-0; *More Forbidden Knowledge* by Matt Forbeck, copyright ©
2009 by Gusto Company AS, ISBN 10: 1-60550-032-1, ISBN 13: 978-1-60550-032-
4; *Forbidden Knowledge: Travel* by Michael Powell, copyright © 2009 by Gusto
Company AS, ISBN 10: 1-4405-0199-8, ISBN 13: 978-1-4405-0199-9; and *Forbidden
Knowledge: College* by Michael Powell, copyright © 2010 by Gusto Company AS,
ISBN 10: 1-4405-0457-1, ISBN 13: 978-1-4405-0457-0.

Many of the designations used by manufacturers and sellers to distinguish
their product are claimed as trademarks. Where those designations appear in
this book and F+W Media was aware of a trademark claim, the designations have
been printed with initial capital letters.

Photographs by BigStockPhoto.com and Istockphoto.com.
Illustrations by Allen Boe and Istockphoto.com.
Design by Allen Boe.

This book is available at quantity discounts for bulk purchases.
For information, please call 1-800-289-0963.

INTRODUCTION

When it hits the fan, what do you want to know how to do? Tie a tie? Iron a shirt? Shave your mustache? Didn't think so. What's really going to come in handy is everything you're not supposed to know how to do. And lucky for you, this is where you're gonna learn how to do it.

From staging a coup and robbing a bank to surviving a plane crash and escaping from prison, this ultimate self-destruction manual shows you how to really bring it. Whether it's going on the offensive by knocking someone out, or getting together a good defense to protect against a tiger attack (or just getting whatever you want by swiping someone's credit card), *The Most Forbidden Knowledge* teaches you how to survive and thrive in this chaotic world. Because when it comes down to it, it's up to you to get yourself ahead.

You'll find out how to deal with extreme scenarios as well as how to give yourself an edge in everyday life. The how-tos that follow are an education in intensity. So whether you're in search of the next great adrenaline rush or in need of an innovative escape plan, there's plenty to learn. Now sit back, buckle up, and enjoy the ride.

CONTENTS

1. Start a Riot — 8
2. Become an Assassin — 10
3. Cheat on Your Partner — 12
4. Free Dive Competitively — 14
5. Escape from Prison — 17
6. Drill a Hole in Someone's Skull — 19
7. Crash a Wedding — 21
8. Smuggle Live Animals — 23
9. Beat a Metal Detector — 25
10. Free Climb the Eiffel Tower — 27
11. Chase a Giant Tornado — 29
12. Survive Being Shot — 32
13. Navigate a Minefield — 37
14. Pirate Copyrighted Files — 41
15. Enjoy Bondage — 44
16. Lie Your Way Into the Ivy League — 47
17. Swipe a Credit Card Number — 50
18. Buy and Sell Drugs — 54
19. Live Rent Free — 56
20. Stage a Coup — 59
21. Beat a Speed Camera — 62
22. Become a Mafia Boss — 65
23. Survive an Alien Abduction — 68
24. Rob a Bank — 70
25. Run a Pyramid Scheme — 72
26. Subway Surf — 74
27. Convince People They're Insane — 76
28. Boot and Rally — 78
29. Find a Booty Call — 80
30. Cheat Your Way Through Exams — 82
31. Buy on the Black Market — 85
32. Venture Into Mayan Ruins — 89
33. Find Atlantis — 91
34. Survive a Plane Crash — 93
35. Become a Mercenary — 97
36. Summon a Demon — 100
37. Survive a Disaster — 103
38. Disappear — 105
39. Launder Money — 107
40. Breathe Fire — 109
41. Become a Porn Star — 112
42. Build an Atom Bomb — 116
43. Negotiate with Kidnappers — 119
44. Bullfight — 121
45. Perform Open Heart Surgery — 124
46. Count Cards at a Casino — 127
47. Screw Up Someone's Car — 131
48. Climb the Pyramids — 134
49. Find the Ark of the Covenant — 137

 50. Hunt a Yeti in the Himalayas —————————————— 140
 51. Claim Political Asylum————————————————— 142
 52. Play with Booze and Fire ——————————————— 146
 53. Knock Someone Out ————————————————— 149
 54. Amputate a Limb ——————————————————— 151
 55. Practice Gun Fu ——————————————————— 153
 56. Get Hit by a Car and Survive ——————————— 155
 57. Make a Shiv ————————————————————— 157
 58. Kite Checks ———————————————————— 159
 59. Avoid Bounty Hunters ———————————————— 161
 60. Get Rid of a Body ————————————————— 163
 61. Chemically Enhance Your Athletic Performance ———— 164
 62. Saw a Woman in Half ——————————————— 166
 63. Play Russian Roulette ——————————————— 169
 64. Beat a Lie Detector Test —————————————— 172
 65. Commit Identity Fraud ——————————————— 175
 66. Counterfeit Money ————————————————— 177
 67. Create Crop Circles ———————————————— 179
 68. Make Moonshine —————————————————— 182
 69. Walk on Hot Coals ————————————————— 185
 70. Sell Your Organs for Beer Money —————————— 187
 71. Construct and Use a Beer Bong —————————— 189
 72. Grow Marijuana in Your Room ——————————— 191
 73. Con Your Way Into the Space Program ——————— 194
 74. Talk Your Way Past a Border Guard ————————— 196
 75. Go Over Niagara Falls in a Barrel ————————— 199
 76. Have Underground Cosmetic Surgery in Brazil ——— 201
 77. Kill Your Computer ————————————————— 203
 78. Become a Religious Icon ————————————— 205
 79. Light a Fart on Fire ————————————————— 208
 80. Avoid Ridiculous State Laws ——————————— 210
 81. Go BASE Jumping ————————————————— 214
 82. Become a Fake Medium —————————————— 217
 83. Break Bricks with Your Hands —————————— 220
 84. Exercise Your Squatter's Rights ————————— 222
 85. Sneak Into Mecca ———————————————— 224
 86. Fly for Free ——————————————————— 226
 87. Smuggle Illegal Immigrants in Your Truck ———— 229
 88. Land an Airplane in Open Water ————————— 232
 89. Eat Blowfish in Japan —————————————— 234
 90. Kill a Vampire ————————————————— 236
 91. Beat a Breathalyzer ——————————————— 239
 92. Restart a Stopped Heart ———————————— 242
 93. Challenge Someone to a Duel ————————— 245
 94. Survive in a Foreign Jail ——————————— 247
 95. Become a Computer Hacker ——————————— 250
 96. Make a Perfect Getaway ———————————— 252
 97. Go AWOL from the Armed Forces —————————— 254
 98. Sleep with Your Professors ——————————— 256
 99. Get Into Secret Societies ——————————— 258
100. Run a Wet T-shirt Competition —————————— 260
101. Avoid Being Scammed by a Bartender ——————— 263

102. Pass a Drug Test — 266
103. Get a Fake Passport — 269
104. Join an Anti-Whaling Crew — 272
105. Get Bumped Up to First Class — 274
106. Become a Snake Charmer — 277
107. Street Race in Malaysia — 279
108. Break Into a Panda Reserve — 281
109. Be a Drug Mule — 283
110. Land a Plane in Red Square — 286
111. Swim with Sharks — 288
112. Lie Effectively — 290
113. Stow Away on Board a Ship — 292
114. Be a Sex Tourist — 295
115. Waterboard a Terrorist — 297
116. Cheat at Gambling — 300
117. Get Out of Handcuffs — 302
118. Start Your Own Fraternity — 305
119. Get Served Underage — 308
120. Throw a Kicking Keg Party — 313
121. Survive in the Australian Outback — 316
122. Traffic in Cultural Antiquities — 319
123. Have Sex on a Beach — 321
124. Start a Motorcycle Gang — 323
125. Protect Against a Tiger Attack — 325
126. Perform an Exorcism — 327
127. Perform a Handbrake Turn — 329
128. Make College Last Forever — 331
129. Elevator Surf — 333
130. Swim with Piranhas — 335
131. Go Whoring in Tangier — 337
132. Drive Your Neighbor Away — 339
133. Pick Someone's Pocket — 341
134. Sober Up Quickly — 344
135. Travel to Volatile Countries — 346
136. Find a Hidden Tribe in the Amazon — 348
137. Tell if Your Neighbor Is a Zombie — 350
138. Break Into a Car — 353
139. Shoplift — 356
140. Have a Kidney Transplant in the Philippines — 359
141. Track Down the Most Poisonous Animals — 361
142. Break 200 MPH on the Autobahn — 364
143. Travel to the Future — 366
144. Hang, Draw, and Quarter — 369
145. Place a Gypsy Curse — 371
146. Streak at a Sporting Event — 373
147. Ward Off Evil Spirits — 375
148. Build Freakish Muscles — 377
149. Hitchhike from LA to NYC — 379
150. Join the Mile High Club — 381
151. Become a Cliff-Diving Thrill Seeker — 383

1. Start a Riot

Sounds like a tall order, huh? Not really. It's very easy to manipulate a group of people if you know something that they don't, and it only takes a few individuals to define the situation for everyone else. Of course, the best thing about a riot is that you get to break stuff and loot.

1. Get a bunch of your friends to dress as Los Angeles cops, then video them kicking the crap out of a black taxi driver. Post the footage on YouTube and watch the sparks fly.

2. Go to a march in Seattle and start smashing store windows. Soon local criminals will join the fray and start looting the downtown shops. The police will be poorly prepared and understaffed, and will be unable to stop the looters from running amok. Under pressure from federal officials, the city will declare an emergency and call in the National Guard.

3. Assemble a group of friends, dress up as activists, and attend a demonstration where there are lots of hard-core nuts, like animal rights protesters. Then get a couple of braver friends (who are dressed as police officers) to start pushing you around at a prearranged signal, using

unreasonable force. This will get the crowd jittery, so that the moment one of the "cops" accidentally kicks your dog, or steps on your hamster (which you have conveniently left on the ground), violence will erupt on the streets, and within half an hour you'll be enjoying a roaring spectacle as water cannon meets Molotov cocktail.

4. Go to a funeral service for victims who died in the last riot. There will be lots of tears and sobbing as well as rage and anxiety desperate for an outlet. All you have to do is throw a brick into a crowd of mourners and the whole thing will kick off.

5. Get a job in Starbucks in New York City. Wait for a killer heat wave and then offer free iced coffee to the first hundred customers.

2. Become an Assassin

All you need to get started in the tough and glamorous world of contract killing is to place a classified ad that euphemistically expresses your gun-for-hire credentials. It is well-known in underworld circles that 60 percent of pest control adverts are actually selling the services of hit men: "Professional pest control: we have been helping homeowners, busi-nesses, and deranged oligarchies solve their extermination problems since 1972. Send a manila envelope with your details to . . . dis-cretion is our profession . . ."

When your first assignment comes in one morning, you're in business; it's time, as they say in hit man circles, to "go to work."

Rifle Assassination

Your method of dispatching your target will depend on the weap-ons that you keep under your bed (all thanks to the Second Amend-ment). If you have a rifle, you can stay concealed and shoot from a distance; if you've only got a pistol, then you'll probably need to pose as a delivery person and gun them down when they open their front door wearing their pajamas. Any assassin who wants to be taken seriously should own a range of weapons, so we'll assume that you have a rifle.

The first rule of rifle assassination is to stay concealed. This means masking shiny or reflective items on your body and face (follow a regular skin-care regime to avoid oily patches), and eliminate unnecessary movement. Always go to the bathroom before a hit—you may not have another opportunity for several hours.

There are six basic positions of concealment: above, below, beside, behind, inside, and in front. Beware of silhouetting when you're on a roof or of getting trapped (never move into a space with only one escape route).

Aiming Your Rifle

Grip the handle with your right hand and bring it up to your face. The rifle should be parallel to the ground. Place the barrel in your open left hand and then curl your fingers around it. Keeping the left arm bent and the elbow tucked into the body, raise the right elbow so that your arm is parallel with the ground, and tuck the rifle butt into the front of your right shoulder. Take aim.

Allow for the influence of wind and other factors that affect the fall of the bullet. Breathe steadily and normally, and do not hold your breath as you squeeze the trigger.

Keep Practicing

Buy a video game system and practice killing for money: there are lots to choose from including *Oblivion*, *Hitman 2: Silent Assassin*, and *Assassin's Creed* to name but three.

3. Cheat on Your Partner

Whether you are a man or a woman, it's time to face the fact that monogamy is unnatural. Sexual fidelity is virtually nonexistent in nature (sure, some species, mostly birds, are socially monogamous, but few are sexually monogamous). We all come from a long line of successful breeders and it is hard-wired into our genes to play away from home. Did you know that 85 percent of human cultures before the Judeo-Christian homogenization were polygamous? So what's the best way to do it?

1. The most important rule is DON'T GET CAUGHT. Cheated-on partners can do some extreme things when they discover they've been duped.

2. Don't date two people in the same city, otherwise you're bound to bump into one while out on a date with the other.

3. When you're on a date, always answer your cell phone; ignoring calls is a quick route to raising suspicion.

4. Develop a reputation in your relationships of being a bad liar; allow yourself to get caught lying badly over something trivial and your partner won't suspect that you could give lessons to Richard Nixon.

5. Be prepared for double-dating to take up twice your energy; eat healthily and exercise regularly: you'll need every bit of stamina you've got.

6. If you're living with your partner, never bring your affair home, as alien pubes in the soap dish or between the sheets are a dead giveaway.

7. When covering your tracks, always base your lies on the truth and pay attention to small details. Also, don't lie unless absolutely necessary: if you lie all the time, no one will believe you.

8. If your partner suspects that you're lying, burst into tears or break something.

9. Don't be tempted to spill the beans if your partner suggests a threesome or swinging; it may be a trap to make you fess up to your cheating.

10. If your partner discovers you've been cheating and you can't see yourself spending the rest of your life together, it is the ideal time to break free and get out. There's no point acting all repentant and spending months trying to rebuild trust for a relationship with no long-term future.

4. Free Dive Competitively

Bronzed streamlined bodies in the tightest fitting wetsuits imaginable descend to the depths of the ocean to see how long they can hold their breath before the light at the end of the tunnel tells them it's time to return to the surface. If you prefer holding your breath and journeying to the outer limits of consciousness to sitting in the bar drinking a beer with your friends, here's how to get started.

1. Watch Luc Besson's dreamily ambient movie, *The Big Blue*, starring Jean Marc Barr as a mystical loon who falls in love with Rosanna Arquette and then dumps her for a dolphin. If that movie doesn't make you hanker for the depths, nothing will.

2. Competitive free diving is currently governed by two world associations: AIDA International and CMAS. There are several disciplines to try out to find which suits you best:

Static apnea: timed breath holding in a swimming pool

Dynamic apnea: underwater swimming in a pool for distance; can be done with or without fins. There are six depth disciplines, which differ in the method of descent and ascent, of which "no limits" is the most sexy: you use any means of breath-holding to dive to depth using a weighted sled and return to the surface along a guideline with the help of an air-filled bag.

3. Meet other free divers to learn more about the sport, join an online discussion group, and go to the pool to practice.

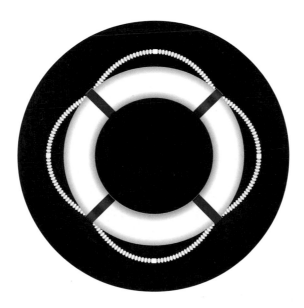

Training

Fortunately, humans have the mammalian diving reflex. That means as soon as you dive to depth you will experience a drop in heart rate; your blood vessels will shrink and fill up with plasma to prevent your lungs from collapsing; and blood is directed away from the limbs to the heart, lungs, and brain.

One training method is the apnea walk. First you spend time spinning your chakras and getting all Zen, then take a few deep breaths, followed by a one-minute breath-hold taken at rest. Then you walk as far as you can without taking a breath (top free divers can walk for over 400 meters). This trains your muscles to operate under anaerobic conditions and to tolerate the buildup of carbon dioxide in the blood stream.

Hyperventilating before a dive lowers the level of carbon dioxide in your lungs and bloodstream, which fools your body into thinking that it is less starved of oxygen than it really is. However, it doesn't raise the amount of oxygen, so most free divers only take three or four oxygenating breaths before a dive.

Always train and dive with a friend. Diving alone is the main cause of serious accidents. If you black out, you need a friend to drag you back to the surface and give you the kiss of life.

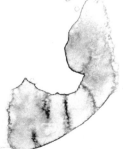

5. Escape from Prison

Only consider a jail break if you are on death row or serving a life sentence with little chance of parole. Otherwise, you would be wiser to do your time, unless conditions inside have become intolerable for other reasons, such as your having recently become another prisoner's bitch or your broker needs a signature before he can offload some more pharmaceutical shares. It is worth considering the consequence of a failed escape attempt: solitary confinement, an increase in your sentence, or drowning in the freezing waters of San Francisco Bay.

Methods of Escape

If you are disorganized or lack the necessary temperament to plan and execute a getaway over several months, you would be more suited to an opportunistic escape: a door left unlocked, a faulty electric perimeter fence, etc. However, you may have to wait a long time for such an opportunity to present itself, time better spent tunneling a hole behind the toilet. Also, if you consider that the odds of one door being left unlocked is a hundred to one, then if you have to get through five doors to reach freedom, your chances of all five of them being unlocked at the same time is one in ten billion. To put this into perspective: you're two million times more likely to die in the first thirty days after a total knee replacement surgery.

If, on the other hand, you are a meticulous planner, good with your hands, and a perfectionist problem-solver with an eye for detail like Martha Stewart, you should opt for a planned escape. If nothing else, your single-minded focus on breaking out will give you a sense of hope and purpose that is so often lacking in correctional facilities.

Getting Help

Whether you dig a tunnel, hide in a laundry sack, or start a riot, most prison breaks require assistance from others either inside or outside the prison. Those on the outside—friends and family—you can trust. However, getting people to help you in prison requires considerable interpersonal skills, and you must be prepared to forgo some of your luxuries (e.g., your toilet paper and cocaine ration) so that you can use them to bribe other inmates or even a prison guard to assist you and to keep quiet.

Plan B

If your escape plan fails, just continue to be clothed, fed, and housed by the state until massive federal budget cuts force the release of hundreds of prisoners.

6. Drill a Hole in Someone's Skull

If you or a loved one has become possessed by an evil spirit or demon that is causing an illness or disease of some kind, your first step is to thrash, starve or torment the individual in an attempt to drive the spirit out to search for a more hospitable host. If that fails and their condition persists, you may be forced to follow the lead of generations of ancient man: trepanning. This is a process by which a section of the top of the skull is carefully removed so as to promote mental and physical well-being.

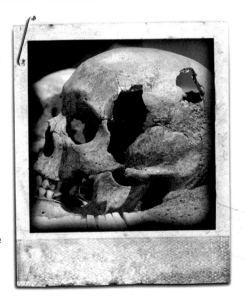

The ancients used trepanning with some success: many skulls show that the bone continued to grow around the hole, indicating that the patient did not die from the procedure. Trepanning was used for centuries to treat conditions as varied as common headaches to epilepsy and more serious mental disorders. With the advent of modern power tools and drugs, this procedure is considerably easier than it used to be.

Here's what you do:

1. Concoct an ointment from herbs that are known to have a mild anesthetic quality, for example kava kava.

2. Apply the ointment generously to a small area at the top of the skull.

3. Cut away a flap of skin with sharp flint tools and fold back; do not cut away completely as you will need this later.

4. Make a series of small round holes in the skull with a power drill so that you have traced the outline of a small circle (if you want to be more traditional and "unplugged," use a hand-cranked drill specifically designed to pierce the skull).

5. Cut between these holes with a pair of pruning shears until you have removed a section of the top of the skull completely.

6. Pay careful attention not to cut too deeply: you are not aiming to remove brain tissue, simply bone.

7. After surgery, stitch back the skull and cover with a sterile gauze to prevent infection. Allow your patient several months to recuperate.

7. Crash a Wedding

There are three common reasons for attending a wedding without an invitation: stealing food, getting laid, and mingling with celebrities. You may even hit pay dirt with the holy grail of wedding crashers: lucrative paparazzi shots.

Stealing Food

This is probably the least ambitious motivation for the wedding crasher, and may not even be cost effective. If you've had to spend several hundred dollars on an outfit to blend in with the wedding party, it is unlikely that you can recoup your initial expense, no matter how many salmon terrines you manage to stuff into your handbag. If a free meal ticket is your main goal, hit low-budget, low-class weddings, and accept that instead of lobster thermidor and caviar you are more likely to encounter quiches, sausages on sticks, and deviled eggs. On the plus side, there's no need to hang around for the wedding speeches. In a high-class wedding, pretend to be one of the caterers, because after you've spent eight hours on your feet serving, you'll get to finish off the vol-au-vents and other uneaten high-brow food (of which there will be plenty).

Getting Laid

Everyone knows that weddings are the place to get laid by horny bridesmaids. Dressing up a pretty young single woman in pink crinoline and forcing her to watch her best friend joined in holy matrimony is a surefire recipe for making her feel unloved and over-the-hill. That's why all bridesmaids are up for it, but it's also why you should avoid them: every other guy in the place will be hitting on them, leaving all the other females to fall for your charms.

The Celebrity Wedding

Don't feel guilty about crashing a celebrity wedding. Sell your photographs to a national glossy magazine and every-one benefits: the magazine pays you a fortune, its circulation increases by a couple hundred thousand, and the celebrity couple sues them for $2 million for stress, loss of income, and damage to their professional careers.

Three Wedding Crashing Tips

Now you know *why* crashing a wedding is good news, here are three hows:

1. Wear a kilt if you're a man, or take along a baby and breastfeed it if you're a woman.

2. If the wedding clashes with an important sporting event, bring a portable radio and keep the male guests abreast of the score.

3. If you sit in Madonna's seat, don't pretend to be Madonna.

8. Smuggle Live Animals

People love pets. People especially love exotic pets. Help people get what they love by smuggling exotic pets into the country. There's many different ways to get all sorts of animals by those pesky custom officials. You just have to get creative—and be ballsy. Whether you dare to walk through the airport with a monkey posing as a toupee or with a snake coiled around your chest, it's up to you. Exude confidence and you'll be all set . . . right?

Here's a list of some of the most sought-after exotic animals:

1. **PYGMY MARMOSET:** The smallest of all monkeys, it's native to the South American rainforests and could double as a toupee or possible tuft of chest hair if you plan on picking one up and flying it back to the States.

2. **SHINGLEBACK SKINK:** A short-tailed lizard that lives in Australia, its rough skin will cause some issues when you try to shove it down your pants to get it past airport security.

3. KEEL-BILLED TOUCAN: What better way to enjoy your morning Fruit Loops than with a live toucan perched on your kitchen counter? Apparently this is how a lot of people want to start off their days as these exotic birds are in high-demand. Road trip it to Bolivia and purchase one from a street vendor for cheap. Drive back up and sell it for big bucks.

4. SNOW LEOPARD: Head over to the Himalayas and see about coming into ownership of a baby snow leopard. These spotted wild cats can catch quite a price at an illegal exotic pet auction. Take your tabby with you when you head over to Asia, and swap him out with the leopard—hoping your old cat's custom forms work for your new acquisition.

5. ROCK PYTHON: Travel to any African country south of the Sahara and see if you can purchase a rock python from any of the local vendors. You'll most likely be able to pay pennies for the snake that will make you some major scratch back home. In terms of getting home—wrap the snake around your torso and waltz right through security. Just be careful things don't get a little too tight.

9. Beat a Metal Detector

Metal detectors have been a standard fixture in airports since the '60s and within the next ten years they will be replaced by full-body scanners, so get your kicks while you can.

How Metal Detectors Work

Almost all airport metal detectors use pulse induction (PI). The detector sends out a short but very powerful pulse of electricity which creates a brief magnetic field. By measuring how quickly the magnetic field collapses, the detector can tell whether metal is present. The magnetic field lasts a fraction longer when it encounters metal, similar to the way a sound wave will bounce off a room with metal walls, and cause an echo.

Asbestos

Some sources claim that it is possible to conceal metal objects in an asbestos sheet, rubber, or concrete. This is supposed to stop the magnetic field from reaching the metal, but since airports also use X-ray machines, these materials would show up as anomalies.

In theory, it ought to be possible to create an electronic device that would cloak metal objects by neutralizing where the magnetic field comes into contact with the metal, but that's CIA stuff, and would take a whole book to explain, even if we knew how. Diplomatic pouches are a much easier low-tech solution to this problem.

CIA Glass Gun

In the movie *In the Line of Fire*, John Malkovitch makes a gun out of plastic and manages to smuggle it in pieces past a metal detector; in *Die Hard II*, it's a ceramic gun (a fictional "Glock 7"). There has been a lot of buzz surrounding non-metal weapons in the media as well. A story appeared in the *Washington Post* in 1985 entitled "Quaddafi Buying Austrian Plastic Pistol," but currently the technology to make guns out of plastic and ceramics still doesn't exist in the public domain.

It is highly likely that secret hi-tech materials with the strength and functionality of metal have been developed by the military and secret services, or poached from industry—an article in a 1995 issue of *Modern Gun* discussed rumors that the CIA had appropriated a new material developed by General Motors for its exhaust valves. It also talks about a "glass gun" made out of ceramics. However, this is all very hi-tech, so the best you can do is get something like the Glock 17, which when stripped down can only be spotted with special training. Your bullets would have to be non-metal too, unless you conceal them in a rabbit's foot key-ring.

POLICE NA
Aéroport de
26 NOV. 1
FRANCE

10. Free Climb the Eiffel Tower

The iron tower completed on the Champ de Mars beside the Seine River in Paris in 1889 is one of the most famous manmade objects in the world. During its lifetime, the 1,063 foot structure has been visited by more than 200 million people, making it the most visited monument with an admission fee on the planet. Evidently, if you want to stand out from the crowd, you need to do something unique on your visit—like scale it without ropes.

Urban Climbing

Who hasn't at some time or other shimmied up a drainpipe when they forgot their house keys? How hard can it be to climb the Eiffel Tower? Read *With Bare Hands*, written by the talented nutcase and "Human Spider," Robert Alain, the most famous and successful free climber in the world. You'll be good to go after gleaning some pointers from his mixture of climbing philosophy ("Man creates his own limitations, but we all have within us the strength to overcome to achieve our goals.") and practical tips, such as carrying a small pouch of chalk to dip your hands in.

The Ascent

The tower is split into three levels. You can reach the first two by stairs (347 steps to the first level, 327 steps to the second level) and elevators, but the top of the third level is only accessible to the public by elevator, or in your case, free climbing. It will save you 12 Euros—barely enough to buy an overpriced espresso and croissant on the Champs-Elysées— so don't attempt the climb just to save money. You'll get arrested and fined afterwards anyway.

Tips for Death-Free Urban Climbing

1. Cut your fingernails.

2. Buy some good quality climbing shoes.

3. Don't look down, except when tying your shoelaces.

4. Don't climb when it's wet—surfaces become too slippery.

5. Only climb structures that support a load, not ornamental features.

6. When resting, straighten your arms and lean back.

7. Climb slowly and methodically.

8. Carry some ID or your dentist's phone number for when you get scraped off the sidewalk.

11. Chase a Giant Tornado

Tornadoes are some of the most violent and dangerous natural events on earth. Every year in the United States, more than a thousand tornadoes spring up; many of them amount to nothing while others tear across the landscape for hours causing mayhem and destruction. A few really rare tornadoes obliterate whole communities. Next summer, take a three week vacation in the central plains and go storm chasing.

What Is a Tornado?

Tornadoes are rotating columns of air that extend from the ground to the cumulonimbus clouds in the sky. Warm humid air at ground spins as it rises and meets colder air higher up; combine this with a large rotating thunderstorm ("supercell") overhead and you've got the conditions for a killer tornado. About one in a thousand thunderstorms become supercells, and one in six of those generate a tornado. You need to know a lot about the weather, or hang around with someone who does to stand a chance of getting up close to a tornado, and doing so safely.

When and Where

In the U.S., about 40 percent of tornadoes appear in the central plains between March and July. Boulder, Colorado—at the foot of the Rocky Mountains—makes a good base camp because you can see for hundreds of miles across the plains, spot the supercells, and drive right to the action.

Technology and Experience

Tornado chasers drive around in vans that are packed with antennae and satellite dishes and they have banks of screens, computers, and satellite-linked televisions to help them predict what's happening with the weather. The successful ones are also staffed with incredibly experienced people. You can't just jump in a pick-up and head for the nearest storm clouds because you'll put yourself in extreme danger. Don't chase tornadoes on your own. You'll reduce your odds of seeing one and increase your chances of getting injured.

For your first season, try to hook up with a seasoned storm chaser; they are hard to find, because they are outnumbered by newbies like you. Otherwise, follow one (they hate that)! Another option is to book a packaged "tornado safari" with a tour firm of skilled chasers; these include Silver Lining Tours, Tempest Tours, or Cloud 9 Tours.

Get Used to Truck-Stop Catering

You will cover hundreds of miles, and the rest of the time you'll be sitting around snacking on truck-stop food waiting for things to kick off. On the road, your biggest dangers aren't tornadoes; they are more mundane threats such as aquaplaning, crashing, or being struck by lightning. Most likely, you won't even see a tornado at all, just lots of rain, hailstones, and Twinkies.

12. Survive Being Shot

If you somehow manage to find yourself on the wrong end of an active firearm, you're likely in for a world of pain. Just because you've been shot, though, doesn't mean you're dead. Here are some tips for how to survive.

Don't Get Shot Again

If you're lucky, this was an accidental shooting, and you're surrounded by many scared and apologetic people who want to help you. If that's not the case, do whatever you can to avoid being shot again. If you're too injured to escape or hide, try playing dead. Unless the shooter really wants you dead, he might not waste any more bullets on you.

Call for Help

If the shot didn't instantly kill you, the biggest danger is that shock or blood loss will do you in before anyone else can get to you. Rather than risk that happening while you make your way to the nearest doctor, call 9-1-1 and have them come to you. They should also call the police, which may help you with the problem of the shooter.

- Find the Wound

You're probably in shock or pumped full of adrenaline. You may not even realize just where the wound is, only that you've been hit. If you can, take off any clothing covering the wounded area and check all around. (That shirt's been ruined anyway, and you can use it in the next step.)

Once you find the wound, look for others. You may have been shot more than once. Also, look on the other side of your body from the wound. You may discover that you have an exit wound: another hole in you from where the bullet left screaming through your body.

- Stop the Bleeding

You need to keep as much of your blood inside of you as you can. Apply direct pressure to the wound to stop the flow of blood. Use a cloth for this if you can, but even your bare hand is better than nothing.

If direct pressure doesn't work, try pressing on the artery supplying blood to the area. If that doesn't help either, try a tourniquet. Using a tourniquet might mean sacrificing a limb, but it beats dying.

Leave the Bullet

Unless you're an ER doctor, taking out the bullet will likely do more harm than good. The bullet acts as a partial plug atop the damage it's done to you. If you pull it out, you remove the plug, and the blood might flow even faster.

Get to a Hospital

If you haven't been able to call for help, go find it instead. If possible, have someone else drive. Passing out at the wheel from blood loss can be as fatal as any gunshot.

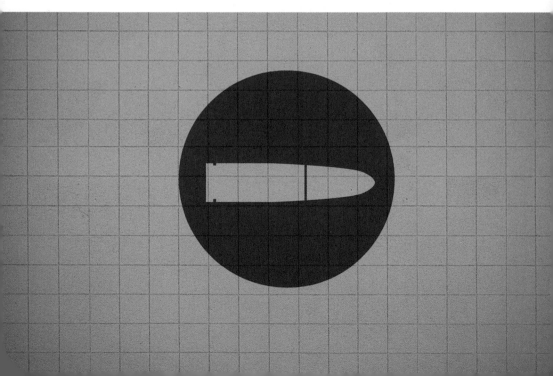

13. Navigate a Minefield

Let's say you're a journalist who's wandering around the mountains of Afghanistan hunting for Taliban to interview. You're hiking up to a remote village and are about to ask your guide how much farther it could possibly be when an explosion sprouts from under his feet and he disappears in a cloud of gunpowder and blood.

You realize that you should have paid for the more experienced guide rather than trying to save your boss a few bucks. Now you're in the middle of a minefield. How do you get out?

Stop Moving

Freeze. Don't make another move until you can assess the situation. A hasty move in any direction could kill you.

Look for a Safe Path Out

The only path you know is safe for sure is where you've already walked. If possible, walk backward into your own footsteps until you are positive you're safe.

If that's not possible, look for another path. You might see where people or animals have successfully negotiated a way through the mines. Stick to these if you can.

Keep Sharp

Peel your eyes for freshly turned dirt, trip wires, spikes, lumps, different soil colors, or other irregularities in the ground around you. Avoid these areas.

Use an Animal

If you have an animal around you, send it the way you figure is the shortest way out of the minefield. Then follow it from a safe distance, stepping exactly in its tracks—or as close as you can manage. This sort of trick only works once per animal though, so take as much care as you can.

Fall Back

Some mines detonate not when you step on the mine but when you step off it. If you step on something and feel it click, you may have found such a mine. In any case, you may have up to a second before the mine goes off. Throw yourself to the ground behind you, your feet toward the expected detonation. You won't be able to outrun the explosion, but you can cover up and protect as much of yourself as possible.

Five Things to Not Do

1. Don't use a probe to find a mine. If you're close enough to set it off, it's close enough to hurt you—or detonate a mine that's closer to you.

2. Don't use a two-way radio to call for help. Their frequencies can detonate some mines. A cell phone might too, although this is less common.

3. Don't voluntarily detonate a mine if you're anywhere near the minefield. You might cause a chain reaction that could kill you.

4. Don't depend on a metal detector. Mines can be made of non-metallic material.

5. Don't try to defuse or disarm a mine—unless you really know what you're doing.

14. Pirate Copyrighted Files

Information wants to be free, right? In one sense, that's true. People who use information want to be able to do so when and where they like, without the troubles that digital rights management (DRM) causes.

For instance, have you every tried to play a song with DRM from iTunes on an MP3 player other than an iPod? It can't be done.

Well, of course it can be done. Just not legally.

Burn and Rip

The easy way around this is to burn a CD of your DRM'd songs. Then you can reinsert the disc and rip the songs off it to your music library just as if they were on a store-bought CD.

This, however, is a pain in the ass.

P2P Networks

Once you're ready to ignore copyright laws entirely and stick it to the RIAA (Recording Industry Association of America), you need to tap into one of the more popular peer-topeer networks out there, like Gnutella or BitTorrent. For this, you just need to grab a program like Acquisition on the Mac, or BitTorrent, or LimeWire on Windows.

Once you get on the P2P Network, just search for whatever you like, from the latest Britney Spears album to your favorite porn films. Then set your program to download the goodies and wait for the files to appear on your computer.

With BitTorrent, you need to find a Torrent file first. Fortunately, there are search engines on the web that make this easy, like ThePirateBay.com. Once you have this file, you simply open it with your BitTorrent client and use it.

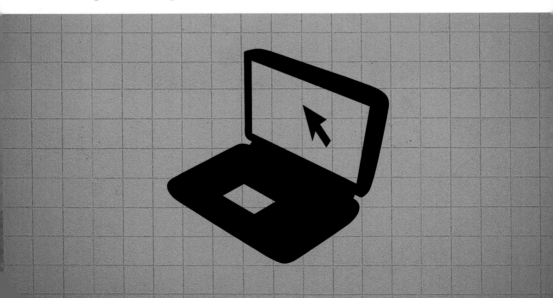

Legal Concerns

While pirates (those who download files illegally) may want information to be free, the same isn't true of those who create that information or publish it. These folks want to be paid for their efforts, and many of them view pirates as direct threats to their livelihoods.

There's an ongoing debate about whether or not freely available files help or hinder actual sales numbers. Despite that, the RIAA and MPAA (the equivalent organization for producers of movies) have taken strong legal action against pirates of all stripes. (Whether or not this is always legitimate or wise is the subject of another set of debates.) Fines can be up to $150,000 for each song traded illegally. Keep that in mind when deciding just how free "free" music might be.

15. Enjoy Bondage

Bondage is technically the use of restraints for pleasure—generally sexual pleasure. It does not have to, but can, include spanking, ball gags, light torture, controlled pain, chocolate syrup, or the all-too-appropriately named whipped cream.

Bondage is not for everyone, but a good and growing number of people seem to enjoy it. If you're thinking of tossing a few ropes or a set of handcuffs into your bed to see what might happen, here are a few tips to get you started.

Start Slow

Don't jump straight into full-leather bodysuits covered with zippers over every orifice and D-rings for restraint clips. Go easy and see how you like it. Start tying each other up with bandanas and work your way up to ropes and handcuffs later on.

(See the entry on how to "Get Out of Handcuffs" if you're not too sure about all this.)

Build Trust

Find a partner you think you can trust and then build that trust over time. It's hard to enjoy bondage if you're really scared that something horrible might happen to you. It's supposed to be for fun, so pick someone who you think you can have that kind of fun with and then take your time to find out if you're right.

Safety First

Bondage, like a lot of sexual play, often features a healthy bit of roleplaying. The one being held might be expected to beg for release and might be pretty convincing about it. To help both people (or everyone!) involved to feel good about this, establish a safe word before you start.

This word should be something that wouldn't normally come up during conversation—especially as part of the kind of talking that goes on during bondage. When anyone says it, the bondage has to end immediately, and those who are bound must be released. Ignoring a safety word is a terrible taboo in bondage. If you violate that trust, you may find it harder to find some play in the future.

16. Lie Your Way Into the Ivy League

Ivy League acceptance is rife with nepotism, favoritism, inconsistencies, and superficiality, so there's always room for one more impostor. Lie about your GPA and SATs and then steal other people's identities to open up potentially unlimited streams of federal funding. The two most famous examples of this are Esther Reed and James Hogue. Reed was arrested in 2008, at the age of 30, after spending a decade attending Ivy League colleges using various aliases and the identity of a missing person. Hogue invented a persona that he knew would appeal to "Princeton admission committee's self-serving mythology of Ivy league diversity, inclusion and merit." Beware: This is a very sophisticated kind of fraud that requires advanced levels of acting skills and maybe even some computer hacking.

Assume an Identity

Look on missing persons websites to find a missing person, presumed dead (but not officially dead), who is approximately the same age as you. (Reed went one better; she gained access through State Police computers to a missing-persons database accessible only to law-enforcement officials.) Use their Social Security Number, name, and birth date to create an alternate persona. When applying for colleges, if anyone gets suspicious tell them that you are in a witness-protection program.

Alternatively, like Hogue, reinvent yourself as a self-reliant multicultural farm boy (Alexi Indris-Santana), "herding cattle by day, reading Plato by night" who presses all the right buttons with elite pseudo-liberals.

Fake Your ACT or SAT Scores

Hack into the ACT or College Board databases and enter a ACT score of 34 and SAT of 2300. Don't make them higher than that otherwise colleges will get suspicious.

Choose Your College

Reed conned her way into Harvard, Columbia, and California State University at Fullerton, and Hogue got into Princeton. Therefore they probably have introduced a vetting procedure so they don't get caught with their pants down again. But allegedly they haven't cooperated with the police, so if they were fooled once maybe they can be again.

Major in Deceit

Choose a major that can teach you more about being the ultimate con artist. Reed majored in Criminology and Psychology, but you might also like to try Law or Drama, since you'll also require sharp acting skills—a police investigator described

Reed as "an excellent impostor to the point of being pathological."

Become an Expert Listener

The best way to hide your real identity is to show exaggerated interest in others. Most people love talking about themselves, so if you become the perfect listener you won't have to give out much information about yourself. According to one source, Reed came across as "very interested in whatever you're doing, she talks to you about you, but provides very little information on her own." Always line up people and information that you can use to your advantage, so that you can leap-frog to other identities and frauds.

Transfer After Your First Year

If fraud pushes you too far out of your comfort zone there is a boring solution. Forget lying your way into the Ivy League. Go to another college first and show dramatic improvement at the college level from your average high school achievements and then apply to transfer to an Ivy League school. Though, where's the fun in that?

17. Swipe a Credit Card Number

People worry about hackers stealing their credit card numbers online all the time. While there's certainly a risk of this, it's miniscule compared to the chance that some minimum-wage clerk will copy down the number off your card when you hand it to her after a good meal.

Skimming a Card

The easiest way to grab a credit card number that's not yours is to work in a restaurant, bar, or other business in which people routinely give you a card and let you walk away with it. While you're out of sight, all you have to do is copy down the card number, expiration date, and Card Security Code (the three or four numbers on the back of the card, near where it's signed).

If you're in a hurry, place a piece of paper over the credit card and rub it with a pencil or a crayon. This mimics the kind of impression that mechanical credit card machines used to take, long before the advent of the magnetic stripe all such cards now use. Just be sure to copy down the Card Security Code too.

Hacking for Numbers

If you're an international hacker, do your best to break into the customer database of a large retail site on the web. While they have the best security, making them the hardest to get into, they also have a treasure trove of credit card numbers for the taking.

If you can't pull that off, consider setting up a key capture program on a public computer instead, perhaps at your local college or at a nearby internet cafe. Once you grab the collected keystrokes, just look for a set of data that looks like credit card information, and you are good to go.

Don't Use It

Stealing someone's credit card information is a serious crime and carries stiff penalties. The best way to get caught is to go on a spending spree, max out the victim's card, and have everything shipped to your house.

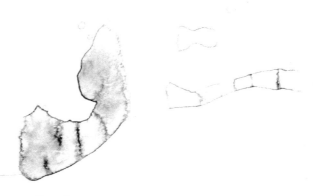

18. Buy and Sell Drugs

In one sense, it's the American dream. See an opportunity and seize it. Find a market and satisfy it. Buy low and sell high.

The only trouble is that the market is illegal, and the product is deadly and ruins lives. But if you don't have a problem with that . . .

Buying Drugs

This is the easy part. There are dozens of people in any decent-sized city who would be happy to sell you drugs if you ask them. There are, of course, some catches. They could rob you, sell you bad drugs, beat you, kill you, and so on.

Most drug dealers won't bother with any of that though. They know the best way to get as much money out of you as possible is to make themselves your new best friend: your supplier. Then they can take you for every spare penny you have over the next several years of your life, until you either get clean or die.

If you're new to buying drugs, just ask around. Most times, the locals in an area know where drugs are being sold, even if they don't know the dealers personally.

— Selling Drugs —

Once you buy enough drugs, if you indulge in them, you'll find yourself addicted to them to some degree. Drugs do not come free, and the more you use them, the more money you blow on them. What better way to make money than to turn your addiction into a business? Start out slow, selling drugs to your friends. Let the word spread from there.

Be careful not to step on the toes of your supplier. If he asks why you're suddenly buying so much more from him, be honest about it. He's going to find out anyhow, and the last thing you want to wind up in is a turf war. This is the perfect time to ask him for a volume discount.

19. Live Rent Free

After tuition and beer, rent is your biggest cost at college, but if you are smart you won't have to pay a cent for your accommodations. There are several possibilities that offer different levels of inconvenience in exchange for free board, from living with your parents to house-sitting a houseboat.

Live with Your Parents

This is the least desirable option for obvious reasons, but if your college is local then it is one way to save money. Only take this route if you really have no other choice, or as a means to an end (like if you are are saving to buy a house/start a business).

Get a House and Rent It Out

Rent or buy a house (getting your parents to act as co-signers) with at least four bedrooms and reserve the smallest room for yourself. Contact the utility company for the cost of running the utilities for a year, then divide the total annual running cost including rent or mortgage payments by 12 to get the monthly budget. Divide this figure again by the number of remaining rooms to get a rough monthly room rent, adjusted up or down depending on the relative size of each room, but making sure that it adds up to your total monthly budget.

Interview tenants, but don't be too picky. Take two months' rent upfront plus a security deposit (put the deposit in the bank and don't touch it) and get them to sign a simple statement of agreement committing them to a minimum of six months. Get Internet, but not a phone account—it's too complicated; everyone can use their cell phones. Rent should be paid on the 1st of each month, it's late by the 5th, and if they haven't paid by the 15th kick them out. Don't cut your price to help someone out, since the most reliable tenants don't ask for favors.

Manage an Apartment

Become the live-in caretaker of an apartment, and you'll live rent free. You will be expected to perform maintenance duties, and will be on call all of the time. Don't tell anyone you're a student. By the time you get sacked you will have saved at least six weeks' rent.

House Sit

Live in someone else's house, sweep the yard, and keep the place clean in exchange for free board. Your length of stay may vary from a few months to a year, so be flexible and you may even be able to skip from one luxurious house to another.

Take Care of a Boat

If your college town has a waterfront, ask around to find a boat owner who needs a responsible, non-smoking, clean person to stay on board to keep it tidy and vandal-free. You could end up taking care of a huge luxury vessel, docked all year round, and you may only have to vacate it for a few weeks each year. Meanwhile, tell everyone the boat belongs to your parents and then ask the gold-diggers who want to hook up with you to form an orderly line.

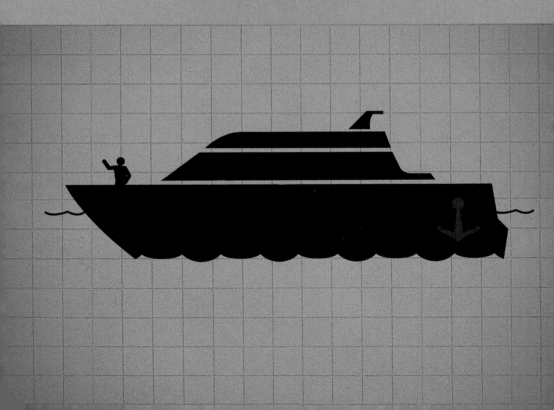

20. Stage a Coup

First decide which kind of coup you would like: bloody or bloodless. As the name suggests, a bloody coup involves a lot of blood, ricocheting bullets, looting, and general mayhem. However, a bloodless coup, though bloodless, is no walk in the park. Both types of coup require you to depose the established government quickly and decisively. You can't maneuver yourself into power simply by baking cookies and offering them to the chief of the military (although this helps).

Choose Your Friends

If your social life consists of hanging around with your posse outside your local fast-food joint arguing about which DVD you are going to rent that evening, then you need to change your social circle. Before you can even think about staging a coup, you've got to get on a first-name basis with large sections of the armed forces, police, or National Guard. Your biggest drinking buddy should be someone like the chief of the armed forces, or, at the very least, a disaffected member of a government agency with access to a large stash of weapons.

Choose Your Country

You can learn a lot about a country from its proverbs. Which of these two countries do you think is ripe for a coup?

Motto A: "Money is power."
Motto B: "Every time a donkey brays, it remembers something."

The answer is, of course, B, typically a small Marxist dictatorship with a population of three million subsistence farmers. Country A is most likely an established capitalist democracy. Stay away from democracies, even small struggling ones, as you'll attract lots of unwelcome air strikes from other countries trying to prop up those in power. However, attacking a Marxist dictatorship will not invite Russian or Chinese hostility, so long as you can persuade them that you are pro-Russian or pro-Chinese.

Cut Above the Neck

Shear off the top layer of government while leaving the old bureaucracy and infrastructure intact but don't do it in haste. For example, if you have arranged for the U.S. Marines to airlift the deposed president out of the country "for his own safety," make sure they do it on the day of the coup. Any earlier looks suspicious.

Control Communications

After the coup, you must control the flow of information in and out of the country. Seize the broadcast and paper media. Put the airport out of action by placing a bomb, car, or herd of goats in the middle of the runaway.

It's a Juggling Act

Convince everyone else in the world that you are pro-them. That means showing democracies that you are pro-democracy (promise to provide for free elections, triple-ply toilet paper, and MTV) while simultaneously persuading autocracies that you are autocratic (free vodka). For example, if your first public act once you're in power is a march past of tanks, karaoke, and cappuccino machines, you will convince everyone that you're the person to be trusted.

21. Beat a Speed Camera

Every year millions of people get fined for speeding. This puts points on their licenses and increases their motor insurance. These fines generate tens of millions of dollars and do little to make the roads safer (since everyone now drives with one eye watching the side of the road to check for speed cameras and brakes heavily when they spot one). Fortunately there are several ways to beat them.

Spray-On Protection

The majority of red light and speed cameras use a strong flash to photograph your license plate. PhotoBlocker comes in a can: you spray it on your plate to produce a high-powered gloss that reflects the light back towards the camera, so that your plate appears overexposed and white on the photo. It is easy to apply and the manufacturers claim that one application is good for at least two years, although you have to polish and wax the plate regularly to maintain a good shine.

Navalert

Invest in one of the many red light and speed camera detectors on the market. Powered by a cigar lighter, they sit on your dashboard and make timely announcements such as "camera ahead limit 60." This gives you plenty of time to slow down and drive like a model citizen. If you don't slow down, you'll even be warned that you are going too fast. You can keep the software up to date via the Internet, by checking on what new cameras are being used, and which ones have been removed. Most devices will also warn you when you are approaching high collision areas and schools, thus improving road safety without you having to part with your cash.

Warp Speed

There is a popular myth that says if you go fast enough through a speed camera it won't react quickly enough to take your picture. The British motoring show Top Gear put this theory to the test. First, the camera clocked a Honda Civic Type-R doing 129 mph. Then a Mercedes CL55 was driven past at 148 mph and was also caught. However, a TVR Tuscan S screamed past the camera at 171 mph without being detected. Conclusion: it's technically possible, but probably not worth the risk or the expense of buying a high-performance sports car.

Beating the Ticket

If you do get caught speeding, you can still beat the ticket:

1. Selective amnesia is your friend. When the speeding fine arrives in the mail, fire back a letter saying you need to see photo proof, because you can't establish who was driving. If they can't identify who was behind the wheel, they can't make you pay.

2. Send a check for a few dollars more than the fine. The system will send you a check back for the difference, but don't cash it. You won't lose demerit points from your license until the financial transaction is complete, so if you tear up the check, it will never happen (this sounds plausible but is probably an urban myth! Still worth a try, though).

Finally, if you really want to beat the system, here's a radical idea you may not have tried yet: don't drive faster than the speed limit.

22. Become a Mafia Boss

Just as you would be unwise to attempt to hang someone upside down and then carve them till they bleed without first locating a sturdy ceiling beam, you'd be absolutely crazy to consider founding your own Mafia dynasty until you own a string

of casinos and brothels, and are deeply involved in money laundering, extortion, drugs, and prostitution. Since the only people who are in that position are already Mafia dons, it begs the question, which came first: the chicken or the cement shoes? In short, the only way to become the next John Gotti is to work your way up from the bottom of a prominent crime family. Yep, it's the same corporate grind whatever career you choose (unless you luck out and land a job at Google—seriously, those guys have gourmet staff restaurants, free laundry, and a petting zoo).

If you do choose a life of crime, remember that the Mafia is not just about guns, money, decapitating horses, and killing people. Being part of the Mafia is a big responsibility to take on. You have to earn trust and respect.

Location, Location, Location

As a member of a criminal fraternity, you will be expected to travel, but you should pick one of these three cities as your base:

LAS VEGAS: Sin City is the gambling center of the world (OK, not counting Macao, which has just overtaken it in terms of total gambling revenue. You want to run the show and didn't know that?). A recent crackdown on organized crime by law enforcement means that other criminal gangs apart from the Mafia have risen to prominence, so you've got even more chance of getting wasted by your rivals. However, with hot summers, mild winters, and abundant year-round sunshine, few places can match up.

NEW YORK: It's got great restaurants and theater, and is home to the big five U.S. crime families: Bonanno, Colombo, Genovese, Gambino, and Lucchese. If you seek the authentic Godfather meets The Sopranos experience, this is the place to go.

CHICAGO: The family in the Windy City, generally known as the "Outfit," has ruled organized crime in the city since the end of Prohibition. It is home to Al Capone, one of the most famous gangsters who ever lived, and is the single greatest symbol of the collapse of law and order in the United States during the 1920s.

Start Breaking the Law

Start with petty theft, stealing cars, and dealing drugs, or, if you are a nerd, start hacking and doing internet scams (electronic crime is BIG business). Your criminal activities will soon attract the attention of the local gang leader (usually a guy called "Fat Tony"). He'll offer to cut you up bad if you don't join his gang, and he'll invite you to shoot someone in a restaurant or dump a body in the river to show that you mean business. Don't mess this up; there's an old Italian saying: "You screw up once, you lose two teeth."

Other Essentials

Learn how to drive, swing a baseball bat, and shoot people (known in criminal circles as "popping a cap up yo ass"). Buy a pair of shades and an 8x10 photo of Frank Sinatra for your nightstand. Always wear shoes with pointy ends and a white hat with a wide black rim, and kiss people Mediterranean style (three cheeks).

23. Survive an Alien Abduction

You're driving your pick-up truck along a deserted road on a clear and still night, when suddenly you see a blinding light in front of you. Your car dies as several gray aliens start gliding towards you. What should you do?

Do Not Panic

Research has shown that 74 percent of potential alien abductees who panic end up scrambling up steep muddy inclines or running through impenetrable forest, only to be zapped unconscious.

Do Not Moo or Chew Grass

Do not do anything that might encourage the aliens to mistake you for a cow, otherwise you will find that your bowels and bodily fluids have been removed before you can say "ruminant mutilation."

Relax

Let's face it—the aliens possess vastly superior intelligence to you and no matter how tightly you clench your sphincter, they will find a way to insert a probe whether you like it or not.

Don't Stand Out

Try to be as boring and "unevolved" as possible. For example, don't start juggling or show them that trick you do with your tongue, or they might think that you are an unusual specimen and cart you back to their galaxy.

Fiddle with Their Stuff

Do you get annoyed when the children start playing with your stereo? When they start pushing buttons indiscriminately, it makes you want to shut them in the garden shed. Well, that's precisely how aliens would react if you started showing a primitive curiosity about their superior technology. Press a few buttons and twiddle a few knobs in the control room. In no time you'll wake up safely in your bed with nothing more than a headache, a sore ass, and a couple of missing hours.

24. Rob a Bank

If you're not comfortable with computers, then holding up a bank the old-fashioned way with a gun and a stocking over your head will net you on average about $7,200 (according to the FBI). You are also more likely to get caught than an identity fraudster who sits at home on his PC and can steal thousands with a few clicks of a mouse. However, if you want to keep a dying art alive, here's what to do.

1. Stake out the bank for several weeks to observe its comings and goings, such as when the staff arrive and leave, when the busy and quiet times are, if there is a police presence, and when large shipments of cash arrive. Locate the surveillance cameras outside the premises.

2. Decide whether to use a real loaded gun, a real unloaded gun, a replica, or a toy gun. If you're caught, each category has different implications on your sentence, but don't assume the courts will be lenient just because you've used a water pistol. Also, if the cops arrive during your heist, you will be shot if you're brandishing any sort of weapon.

3. Better still, wear a dead man's switch that is rigged up to your heartbeat. This will trigger bombs that you have planted previously around the city the moment it detects that your heart has stopped (i.e., when you've been shot dead by the cops).

4. Enter the bank during the quietest time of day; cover your face as you enter, then put on a mask to disguise your face inside.

5. Pass the teller a note with your demands, and tell her to keep her hands in view so she can't press the emergency button.

6. When she has emptied her drawer of bills, stuff them down your pants and leave quickly, making sure that you aren't being followed.

7. Jump into your getaway vehicle, and, if in the unlikely event that you have made off with enough money to live on for the rest of your life, fake your own death and flee to a country that doesn't have an extradition treaty with the U.S.

Identity Theft

Dishonest bank employees will sell the personal banking information of customers for a price that depends on the amount of the funds in the account. If you want to steal millions, the banking details will cost you thousands, so you may have to rob a few banks the old-fashioned way first to build up some capital. Once you've got the bank details, you can take over the account and siphon off large amounts of cash.

Use other people's Social Security numbers and dates of birth to open accounts in their names to launder checks. If the police investigate, it's their names on the accounts not yours.

25. Run a Pyramid Scheme

Pyramid schemes are illegal. They are "get-rich-quick" clubs which offer its members a large return on their investment, so long as they are able to recruit new members. However, these schemes quickly collapse and only those at the top make money. So why not be the one at the top? Here's how.

Exploit Greed and Ignorance

Pyramid schemes don't create money, they merely take it from those recruited later on down the line to pay those at the front of the queue. Fortunately, most people are blinded by greed and ignorance and don't understand that it would take an endless supply of new members to enable everyone who joined to see a return. As long as you don't draw attention to this, you're a winner.

The Letter

A pyramid scheme is the same as a chain letter, only money changes hands. Mail out a letter containing a list of six people's names and addresses (you and five friends) to a hundred people. The letter invites the recipient to "earn a windfall" and contains lots of enticing phrases like "Become part of the world's fastest growing industry" to convince them that this is an opportunity too good to pass over. All they have to do is send one dollar to the person at the top of the list (you), then cross out your name, slide the second person (your friend) to the top position, and add their own name and address in the bottom position. Then they need to copy the letter and send it to five friends. In return they will receive big bucks when their name reaches the top of the list.

The Payoff

Of course, their name will never reach the top of the list, because if they understood statistics they'd realize that 48,828,125 people would have to take part before you and your five friends disappear from the list. Meanwhile, you'll all be busy booking tickets to an exotic destination to spend your hard-earned winnings.

26. Subway Surf

Anyone can take part in the frighteningly dangerous and imprudent sport of subway surfing. Just jump on one of the thousands of trains that make up the New York City subway system, and then ride the waves for a few minutes until you drop to your inevitable death.

How to Surf

The best surfing position is a snowboarding stance: spread your feet a little more than a shoulder-width apart, with one foot slightly in front of the other, and bend your knees.

Your front foot should face the front of the train, and your torso should face the side of the train. Keep equal weight on both feet and stretch out your arms for balance.

Look out for tunnels, bridges, and other overhead obstacles, and watch what the cars ahead of you are doing so that you can anticipate movement (e.g., watch to see if the train will turn left or right suddenly).

The Benefits

1. You don't have to share the roof with anyone else or stick your face in someone's armpit.

2. You won't get pick-pocketed or mugged.

3. You won't have to breathe in other people's germs.

4. It's a great workout for your core abdominal muscles (mainly transverse abdominus and obliques), inner thighs, glutes, quadriceps, and calves.

5. Even people who can't swim can take part.

The Pitfalls

The subway reaches speeds of up to 30 mph. It's hella dangerous; there are no safety harnesses and no instructors, so if you fall off you're probably going to die, or at the very least injure yourself bad. Still, what else have you got to live for?

27. Convince People They're Insane

Gaslighting takes its name from the 1944 film *Gaslight* in which the main character is led to believe she is going mad: Charles Boyer fiddles with the gas lamps in the loft which makes the rest of the lamps in the house dim slightly; when Ingrid Bergman notices, Boyer tells her she is imagining things. Hundreds of movies use similar psychological techniques: Harrison Ford makes Michelle Pfeiffer think she's going nuts in *What Lies Beneath*, and Audrey Tautou in *Amélie (The Fabulous Destiny of Amélie Poulain)* plays a strange young woman who gaslights her local grocer. Here are ten ways to destroy your victim's sense of judgment and make them paranoid.

1. Say hurtful things and make them cry, and then, instead of apologizing start recommending treatments for their depression, mood swings, and low self-esteem.

2. Replace their slippers with an identical pair that is two sizes smaller. Do the same thing with their clothes so that they think they have a weight problem, or with their hat to make them think they have swelling of the brain.

3. Replace all the light bulbs in their house with dimmer ones; less light may encourage depression.

4. Move small personal items so that your victim doesn't consciously notice, but subconsciously feels an increasing sense of unease.

5. Remove an item and then return it to a slightly different place when they have wasted an hour searching for it.

6. Each night add a gallon of gas to the gas tank of their car.

7. Mail pornography to their workplace when they are on vacation. It will be opened by someone else in their absence, undermining their reputation.

8. If your victim is a work colleague, chip away at their productivity. For example, if you work in a factory, change a setting on their machine; in an office, steal vital documents before an important meeting or presentation (sabotage a PowerPoint demonstration by adding spelling mistakes).

9. Move furniture around and tell your victim it has always been that way.

10. To develop a habit of compliance in your victim, always enforce trivial demands and make the cost of resistance appear more damaging to self-esteem than capitulation.

28. Boot and Rally

When you've already enjoyed a major bingefest and there are several pressing engagements on your evening's hectic social calendar, sometimes pulling a boot and rally is the sensible choice. Endorphins are released during vomiting so it feels great too! The alternative may be alcohol poisoning, which can lead to coma, brain damage, or death. Don't make a habit of this though because regular puking eats away at tooth enamel and weakens the cardiac sphincter muscle leading to gastric reflux, which screws up your esophagus causing life threatening ulceration and perforation. So remember boys and girls—always toss your cookies responsibly.

The Finger Method

Assume the position—lean forward with your head facing down. Trigger your gag reflex by pressing your middle and index fingers onto the back of your tongue and wiggle them to tickle the back of your throat. This will make you gag and cough; keep going until your stomach starts heaving. Open your throat as if you were is about to swallow a sword; this sends another signal to your brain that a pavement pizza about to be delivered. You should puke in about two minutes max.

Syrup of Ipecac

This poisoning remedy will have you dribbling on the carpet before you can say Ralph Lauren. You can find it in most first aid kits or at your local drugstore. Take two tablespoons of Ipecac immediately followed by three glasses of water. If you haven't blown your chunks after thirty minutes, take one one more dose and no more.

Mustard and Salt

Dissolve three teaspoons of salt in half a liter of hot water followed by 5 ounces of yellow mustard. Drink down in one gulp and then stand back . . . from everything.

2 Girls 1 Cup

If you mistrust emetics and prefer a more organic barfing experience and you have access to the Internet, type "2 Girls 1 Cup video" into a search engine and enjoy this viral barf-inducer, or check out the dead bodies on Rotten.com.

Stress Vomit

Situations of extreme stress causes the body to go into shock, whereupon it eliminates the stomach contents so that it can focus its resources (i.e. blood flow) on dealing with the crisis. So if your drinking buddy is too squeamish to sample any of the above methods, just kick him hard in the nuts.

29. Find a Booty Call

When you've been painting the town red but can't persuade anyone to come home to help soak your brushes, a booty call is the perfect standby. However, lining up a sort-of-friend who will respond to impromptu requests for sexual favors requires a certain degree of skill, someone whose desire for mutual gratification outside a traditional relationship with no strings attached is not precluded by their resemblance to a sack of armpits.

Rough Trade Off

The booty call is inevitably a compromise between what you desire and what you'll settle for at the end of an evening: too easy and they'll already be grinding their coffee with someone else; too innocent and you'll wake them up; too ugly and they will have been chased into the hills by a pitchfork and torch bearing mob. Your ideal booty should be homely with low self-esteem, and if you're really lucky—no gag reflex or teeth; preferring to stay in, but likely to be awake in the small hours (studying). We're talking here of course about the honor roll student: after years of failing to live up to ridiculously high parental expectations, in college they rebel by filling the emotional void with a succession of meaningless physical encounters. Remember to utter the phrase "I'm proud of you" as you cum over her tits.

Off-Peak

Avoid booty calling at 3 A.M. on a Friday or Saturday—that's peak-time when everyone is doing it. Don't neglect the other five nights of the week, especially Mondays and Tuesdays when there's less competition or expectation that you'll be drunk and desperate.

Booty Grazing

When your tame honor roll student is unavailable there's nothing to stop you playing the numbers with some "booty grazing." Who says that a booty call has to be a call—it can be a text. Fire off a generic booty text to everyone in your address book you soberly marked with a "Y" (those are the ones you won't regret waking up with tomorrow); if none of them text you back, send one out to all those with an "X" beside their names (ugly in the morning); and only if they don't text you back do you resort to those tagged with a doodle of a skull and bones dissolving in a barrel of toxic waste (ugly all the time).

30. Cheat Your Way Through Exams

When cheating during an exam, apart from not getting caught, prior preparation is vital, as well as an ability to stay calm under pressure when a professor is standing two feet away staring hard in your direction. Stay calm, don't look around, and focus on your work.

Smartphone

A recent Common Sense Media poll found that more than half of teens in the U.S. use smartphones and the Internet to cheat at schoolwork and exams. It concluded: "The unintended consequence of these versatile technologies is that they've made cheating easier." No shit. But why stop there? You can use your phone to send answers to friends who are set to take the same test later that day, as well as exchange texts during the exam. Remember to disable keypad tones and put your phone on silent.

iPod

Use your PC to edit the lyrics boxes in your iTunes library, filling them with the dates, facts, and formulas you need for your exam. Then sync your iPod to download the songs, and access the cheat sheets in the exam by listening to the song and then clicking on the center button until the information appears.

Adhesive Tape

Type the cheat information in four-line paragraphs of Arial, font size 8. This is easy to read, but small enough to cram in lots of data. Print out your notes using a toner-based laser printer at maximum resolution. Stick clear adhesive tape over each paragraph, cut out the strips, and then soak them in cold water for a few minutes until the paper peels away easily. The text should now appear on the tape. Stick the tape where necessary (up your arm, on the inside of your thigh, your pen, under your hoodie, inside your belt, inside a charity or friendship bracelet, etc.).

Food and Drink

Anything that contains a label can be customized either on Photoshop or using the adhesive tape method to replace or supplement the nutritional information with cheat data. If you can read Japanese, Korean, or Chinese (or failing that, any foreign language), write your cheat data in one of these languages and even under close inspection it will look authentic.

Friendship Bracelet

Use a set of felt tip pens to decorate a friendship bracelet with a color-coded sequence. This can be used to record the answers to a multiple choice exam, so long as you have already managed to steal the answer sheet, or buy the answers from an older student. A=Black, B=Yellow, C=Red, and so on, depending on how many answer choices there are.

Rubber Band

Take one thick runner band and stretch it to its limit between two nails. Write your information on the band with a black ballpoint pen. Release the tension and the words will shrink to illegible marks, until you are ready to stretch the band (or "bracelet" as it has now become) in the exam to reveal your hidden message.

Hidden Earpiece

A Canadian company called ExamEar offers a range of tiny wireless earpieces and microphones with the slogan "helping students succeed." They can easily be used to communicate with someone outside the exam, but hurry up and buy one before the company gets closed down. If so, look for similar gadgets on amateur spying and espionage websites.

31. Buy on the Black Market

Wherever there's a screwed up economy and a dysfunctional domestic policy, you'll find a thriving black market to match. It offers several services: currency exchange, goods cheaper than those in the legitimate market (often because you don't have to pay taxes); goods that are in short supply; cheap replicas or copies; and illegal items such as sexual services and equipment, drugs, weapons, and explosives.

Currency

Beware of changing money on the streets or with private individuals. Don't flash your wad unless you want to get robbed. When your home currency is strong, carry mainly that; when your home currency is weak, carry the currency of the host country or a strong currency like Swiss francs. If your home currency is unstable, carry both. The safest way to use the black market is to haggle in the local market in the local currency and then at the last minute offer a lower figure in your home currency. High class joints generally won't get involved in this, and if you are just a short-stay tourist the risks of black-marketeering outweigh the benefits.

Copyrighted Media

In many Asian countries you can buy ludicrously cheap copies of movies and music CDs, computer software and video games, as well as consumer electronics such as cell phones and gaming consoles. Buy "region-free" DVDs that can be played back home without special equipment. Never spend more than you can afford to lose. The items should be so cheap that you don't mind taking the risk on them either not working or not being what you think you're buying. There's no warranty or after sales support, and you may have to spend time reconfiguring the software when you get home (such as the 3G settings on your cell) and some will be only Asian and no use to you.

Gas

In European countries where gas prices are high, if you rent a diesel car then you may be able to buy agricultural diesel (known as red diesel) cheaply from a corrupt and/or penniless farmer, or simply steal it between the hours of two and three in the morning. Don't put the stuff into your own car as it will ruin the engine.

POLICE NATIONALE
Aéroport de Paris
26 NOV. 1998
FRANCE

VISA

Replica Watches

Never buy an expensive replica; it's just not worth the money and you should be able to find something similar elsewhere for much less. Replicas differ enormously in quality. At the higher end, the exteriors are almost impossible to distinguish from the genuine product, even down to the manufacturer's logo and serial numbers. However, the insides will be cheap and generic, and will only last anywhere between a few months to a few years.

Designer Clothes

The production of fake designer clothing and sneakers in developing countries is bigger than the manufacture of the genuine articles of some large brands such as Nike, Polo, and Levi's. Quality of fakes differs wildly. Large corporations never tire of warning us that fakes are always inferior to the genuine products, but this isn't always the case: some manufacturers of fakes take pride in making their products better than the overpriced originals. Check out the quality of fabric and the stitching, which should be tight, straight, and regular.

Weapons

The best way to buy illegal weapons is to take a mini-vaca-
tion in Iraq, where you will be able to pick up brand new Glock
9-millimeter pistols, and immaculate, unused Kalashnikovs from
post-Soviet Eastern European countries in the local open-
air grocery stands. Thousands of U.S. weapons intended to arm
the Iraqi Army and police have found their way into the black
market as well; plus, lots of weapons left in unguarded aban-
doned Iraqi military bases will be up for sale. Prices are
rising as sectarian mistrust escalates out of control, so snap
up a bargain now before the country descends into civil war
after the coalition troops have pulled out.

32. Venture Into Mayan Ruins

If you ever read *The Ruins* or saw the movie adaptation, you know that these ancient structures are extremely dangerous places for adventurous Americans to explore. Besides the fact that most of these ruins are archeological sites with very limited access, the ramifications for daring to enter such ancient grounds could be deadly. Seeing as how the collapse of the Maya culture is still heavily debated—there's a chance that the temples and other ruins are haunted. Angry spirits and deadly monsters are just as legitimate of a reason for the civilization's abrupt disappearance as an ecological disaster or foreign invasion, right?

Where to Go

The Maya civilization extended from present-day southern Mexico down to El Salvador and Honduras. Your best bet if you dare to go wandering around the ancient cities is to head off to Belize. Fly into the capital city of Belmopan and then head towards the Guatemalan border. Pay a local to lead you through the Peten rainforest and off the beaten path from the Tikal National Park to some lesser-visited ruins of Caracol. You want to find some ancient remnants that aren't roped off and under constant watch.

What You'll Find

Assuming you survived the rainforest trek and that your local guide did not rob you and leave you stranded, you will now be able to wander through the remnants of one of the largest Maya kingdoms. Caracol contains all the staples of Maya civilization and you should be able to locate a number of the society's typical constructions.

Try to find an observatory. Most tour guides who lead groups through the ruins call out round temples as being observatories. Therefore, if you see a round building, it's an observatory. The Mayas built observatories in order to validate their theories about time as well as celestial bodies and events. In fact, the Maya calendar, based on astronomical observations, is the basis for many apocalyptic 2012 myths. See if you can gain any insight to the end of the world by entering one of these ancient structures. If you do, you can hit up the talk show circuit and make a ton of money.

33. Find Atlantis

In 370 B.C., the Greek philosopher Plato wrote about the lost city of Atlantis in two books, *Timaeus* and *Critias*. He didn't invent the idea though, he drew upon the writings of the Greek ruler Solon, which preceded him by two hundred years. Plato reckoned that the once prosperous island of Atlantis had disappeared under the sea ten thousand years earlier. Before its destruction, he says that it had been a powerful state that ruled parts of Europe and Africa, but the greed of the inhabitants angered the god Zeus, who punished them with violent earthquakes and floods. Scholars have argued that Plato got the dates wrong by mistranslating Solon, and that Atlantis was in fact the Minoan island of Santorini, destroyed by a volcanic eruption in 1470 B.C.

Bimini Road

One of the more implausible Atlantean theories centers on the Bimini Road in the Bahamas, where sunken stone formations were interpreted in the early twentieth century by the psychic Edgar Cayce as being a sunken harbor. Cayce and his followers believed they were re-incarnated Atlanteans, so that further explains his argument against the fact that these formations are naturally occurring beach rock, which have been carbon-dated to between 2,000 and 4,000 years old. As absurd reasons for visiting beautiful places go, you can't get a better one than this.

Cuba

In 2001, a Canadian team of oceanographers placed Atlantis off the coast of Cuba. They discovered strange geometrical formations of rocks spread over eight square miles, and nearly half a mile deep, along with an extinct volcano and fault lines. They prevail that the complex was above sea level until an earthquake 8,000 years ago made it vanish.

Take Your Pick

Other possible locations are off the coast of Cyprus in the Mediterranean Sea, near Indonesia, near Puerto Rico (before it was destroyed by a six-mile-wide asteroid), Sardinia, Finland, the Black Sea, and Turkey.

So basically, pick your vacation destination and you'll be bound to find a local site that claims to be the true Atlantis. Fortunately for you, *Man From Atlantis*, the short-lived science fiction television series that ran for just thirteen episodes and four movies is much easier to track down. You can pick up complete VHS-to-DVD copies on dodgy internet sites for less than $30, or P2P torrents for free.

34. Survive a Plane Crash

There is plenty you can do to improve your chances of surviving a plane crash. In the U.S. alone, between 1983 and 2000, there were 568 plane crashes, of which more than 95 percent of passengers survived. Smoke inhalation and fire accounts for more than a third of fatalities.

Avoid Manmade Fibers

Travel in cotton and natural fibers. Manmade fibers will melt onto your skin in a fire. Also, keep your shoes on during landing.

Have an Escape Plan

Pay attention to the safety instructions at the start of the flight. Take a look around and you'll be amazed how many people aren't listening; their inattention reduces their chances of survival (and yours if they get in your way). Count how many rows of seats there are between you and the nearest exit so that you can find your way in the dark (or in smoke) by touch alone. You may have to trample over the heads of some of these arrogant losers to reach safety.

Get the Safest Seat

Some say the safest seats are over the wing, which are near the exit row, located in the strongest part of the plane. However, if there's an engine fire, it's one of the worst places to sit. Statistically, the safest seats are in the rear, where survival rates are 69 percent as opposed to 56 percent over the wing and 49 percent at the front of the plane. In individual cases, the safest seats depend on how the plane crashes, but knowing where your nearest exit, and/or being close to an exit are your top priorities.

Survive the Impact

Pull the seat belt as tight as possible. There's a good reason for adopting the brace position—placing your head over your knees and holding onto your calves, and getting your upper body as low down as possible—it reduces whiplash and stops you from flying forward and hitting the seat in front of you. (The brace position also protects your teeth so that your corpse can be identified using dental records.) When booking your flight, bear in mind that the brace position is often impossible in an economy seat. Place your feet flat on the floor, farther back than your knees, and wedge something soft under the seat in front to act as a cushion (lots of people break their legs below the knee on impact).

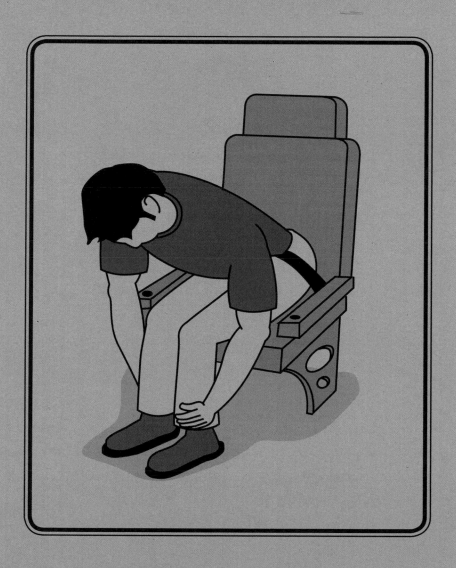

Release the Seatbelt

Flick away; don't press. Many people waste precious time trying to unlock their seatbelt the wrong way. They are used to the push-button release used in cars, and under pressure they revert to this pressing action, when they should be unclasping the buckle by flicking the latch away from them.

Don't Inhale Smoke

Hold your breath or wrap a wet handkerchief around your mouth and nose to filter out some of the smoke (better still, pack a smoke hood in your carry-on). Just a few breaths of toxic smoke can render you unconscious. If you get your eyes and nose at floor level, you will avoid the smoke, but risk getting trampled by other passengers. Keep in mind cabin, floor lights are red, but turn green at the exits.

Listen for Instructions but Don't Wait for Them

Pay attention to instructions from the flight attendants, but if none are forthcoming, don't sit there doing nothing. Those around you may be in shock and will just sit as if stuck in their seats, while others panic and block the exits within seconds. Don't wait. Get moving and calmly head for the nearest exit. Get yourself out. Don't stop to help family and friends or you'll all die.

35. Become a Mercenary

With the perpetual War on Terror in full swing, it's easy to see why soldiers are in high demand—and not just by the governments of the world. Private military contractors (PMCs) fill a real need for extra bodies to take part in various actions, or to act as bodyguards or security professionals in dangerous parts of the world.

But not everyone is qualified to be a soldier of fortune.

Get Qualified

Training with BB guns at Cub Scout camp isn't going to cut it. You need to learn some serious skills, and it's best if you've actually had the experience of putting those skills to use. No one wants to work with an amateur who can get the whole crew killed.

Join a military somewhere. The easiest choice is to sign up with your local army, although they might require a longer term of commitment than you're interested in. If you can get into the special

forces, better yet. The PMCs pay top dollar for people with such qualifications.

You could always try working with a different outfit like the French Foreign Legion instead.

Survive Your Qualifications

Train hard, stay alert, and keep your head down. You can't become a mercenary if you don't live long enough to get discharged from the military. Try for an honorable discharge if you can. The best PMCs don't want to touch anyone with a dishonorable discharge.

Apply

If you're in the military, pay attention to what the soldiers around you do when they leave. Tell them to give you a call when they get set up so they can let you know if life as a PMC is really for you. Then listen to them.

Don't Join Just Any Company

If you join a top PMC, you'll wind up with other professionals who will have your back. If you have little to no qualifications and find someone who will hire you, you'll find yourself with a bunch of yahoos just as unqualified as you. Do you want to have to depend on these people in a firefight?

36. Summon a Demon

If devout prayers or self-help courses and books just aren't doing it for you, you might be tempted to turn to the darkest side there is: demonology. Summoning a demon isn't for the faint at heart, just the soft in head. But if you fall into that category of people and are desperate enough to give it a whirl, here's how to get started.

Pick a Demon, Any Demon

Figure out the name of the demon you want to summon. This is like getting the right phone number. If you dial randomly, you never know who you're going to get, and it's likely not to work at all.

Know What You Want

Demons don't want to be summoned from the netherworld just to chat. Know what you want from your chosen demon, and be ready to cut a deal for it.

Protect Yourself

Draw a circle of protection on the floor. Make it big enough to hold the demon you're summoning. Draw a five-pointed star inside of it, and then place a black candle at each tip.

The circle is supposed to hold the demon like an invisible prison. Don't cross the circle for any reason. And don't place too much trust in how much protection it affords you either. People screw these up all the time. Have a backup plan for your safety or escape.

Set the Mood

Start at midnight. Darken the room. Light the candles. Burn some incense. Then start chanting and petitioning your demon to pop in for a visit.

If You Succeed

If you manage to call on your demon and can replicate your success, call the Smithsonian—or The Enquirer. The world could use some proof.

37. Survive a Disaster

With all the disasters—both natural and artificial—happening around the world these days, it pays to be prepared. You never know when you're going to have to head for the hills and survive on your own for a while.

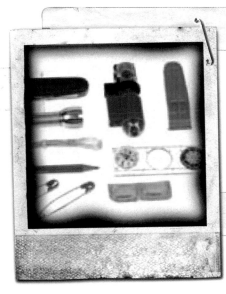

Start Easy

You could build your own survival kit from scratch, but why bother? The Red Cross sells a whole line of emergency preparedness kits online at *www.redcrossstore.org*. These make for a great start, and the money goes to a good cause.

Tailor It

No standard emergency kit will fit everyone's needs. The kits you can buy serve everyone's basic needs, but you know what you have to have better than anybody. Make a list of these things, and add them to your kit.

This includes any medical needs you might have, like:

Prescription medications

Over-the-counter medications

Extra glasses

Extra contact lenses

Extra hearing aid batteries

Also pack any things that might be helpful in your climate. If you live in the desert, put away some extra water, and load up on the sunscreen. If you expect winter trouble, put a coat, hat, gloves, long underwear, and so on, next to your kit too.

38. Disappear

Sometimes you just have to get away. Perhaps you robbed a bank. Maybe you need to leave your wife. Or possibly your stint in the witness protection program has come to an untimely end. No matter what, you need to get away.

1. Leave the country. Go to the airport. Buy a ticket on the next flight to a foreign country. Keep flying until you're far enough away. Then walk into a crowd and fade away.

2. Ditch your old identity. Clean out your bank accounts, max out your credit cards, and run. Leave everything behind and pay for anything you need in cash.

3. Leap out of a perfectly good airplane after hijacking the plane and making off with a cool million in cash.

4. Piss off someone in the Mafia. They have ways of making you wish you'd never appeared in the first place.

5. Volunteer to participate in a magic act.

6. Have your stomach stapled. (Although this only makes you disappear a pound at a time.)

7. Go surfing in the Bermuda Triangle.

8. Fake your own death. This helps throw people off the idea they should be looking for you. You can even leave a suicide note behind for closure of some sort if you like.

9. Piss off the government enough to join in their ongoing extraordinary rendition program. If you do well enough, you may be lucky enough to end up in Gitmo.

10. Run away and join the circus!

39. Launder Money

The trouble with coming into a large amount of money is that people tend to notice. If you suddenly stick thousands of dollars into your personal checking account, bank regulators, the IRS, and possibly the FBI are going to wonder where it all came from.

Laundering money is all about making it look like it came from a legitimate source via financial sleight-of-hand. It's also about converting cash into numbers in a bank account. A million dollars in bills can weigh over 250 pounds, far more than you can fit into a wallet.

Some popular ways to launder money include:

1. Find a compliant bank. Usually you want to use an offshore account for this, in a bank located in a country that has banking privacy laws. Places like the Cayman Islands, Switzerland, Liechtenstein, and Austria are good for this, but transporting large amounts of actual money there can be difficult. Once it's there, though, you can transfer it to more legitimate-looking accounts in other nations and then eventually back home.

2. Overbilling. You establish an import-export business. Overpay a client "accidentally," then request that he deposit the remainder in your offshore account. This works even better if you're providing some sort of service (like consulting) in which no goods have to change hands.

3. Invest in a cash-based service business. Give the money to someone who owns a service-based business that takes in lots of cash, like a barber shop, a plumbing service, construction, delivery services, consulting, and so on. That person deposits the money (while taking a cut for herself) and then puts the rest into the bank. As an investor or owner, you can then withdraw money as a dividend. Or you can bill the business for "consulting services."

4. Set up a personal non-profit. Politicians like Tom DeLay supposedly played this game. As a U.S. congressman, he's not allowed to take corporate donations, but the Republican Nation Committee can. Instead of taking donations directly, his staff directed the donations to the RNC, which then sent him money for his campaign in the exact same amounts.

40. Breathe Fire

Fire breathing is one of the most dangerous stunts you can pull. Even if you don't manage to set yourself on fire, there's always the threat of accidentally drinking the fuel you ignite, which can be just about as bad.

Plus there's always the chance you'll make a mistake and hurt your audience.

Still, if Gene Simmons can pull it off during a KISS concert, then maybe you can too.

How It Works

Fire breathing is simple, although it takes practice to get it right and to be safe. It's only three steps.

1. Fill your mouth with something very flammable.

2. Hold a burning torch in front of you at arm's length.

3. Then, pursing your mouth like a trumpeter and cocking your head back, spray the fluid in your mouth at the torch and past it.

Voila! Gouts of flame that would put a dragon to shame.

What You Need

While you can use lots of things for fire breathing fuel, you shouldn't. Pure ethanol is an easy choice, but you can absorb in into your body without even drinking it. Being intoxicated and playing with fire is a bad mix.

Methanol or gasoline and other petroleum-based fuels work too, but they're all extremely toxic. Even small amounts can make you ill, and some of them are carcinogenic as well.

The best choice is purified lamp oil. This burns at a lower temperature and is easy to ignite.

For a torch, you can make your own or find them through various suppliers.

Your torch should have a metal handle wrapped in leather or some other insulating material, and the wick wrapped on the end of it should have enough integrity that it will not fall off when burning.

Safety Tips

1. If performing outside—as you should unless you have a building with very high ceilings, like an arena or gym—pay close attention to the wind direction and speed. A sudden gust can ruin your whole day. Use your burning torch as an indicator.

2. Wipe your mouth between stunts, especially if you have any facial hair.

3. Don't breathe any of the fuel into your lungs, and don't swallow it either.

4. Blow hard. If you let the fire travel back up the spray and into your mouth—known as blowback—you're in for some serious hurt. Practice with water until you can get a good, strong spray.

5. Pay attention to everything around you. Note nearby trees and power lines. Make sure your audience stays a safe distance away, especially if there are children watching.

6. Have a plan if something goes wrong. Keep a cell phone with you so you can call for help. Arrange for a fire blanket or a hose to be nearby in case something accidentally catches on fire. Always have a good-sized fire extinguisher with you too.

7. Check with your local fire department about permission for performances. Work with them to come up with a safety plan.

8. Train with a partner—or at least a spotter. Have this person around when you perform too. Someone has to be ready to put you out and call 9-1-1.

41. Become a Porn Star

Girls have an easier time getting into porn than men. If you're a woman with a nice face and body (a 6 or above on the 1 to 10 scale), then you can go to Los Angeles for a week and make two movies a day if you want, then go home with a wad of cash. Guys, on the other hand, have to live in Los Angeles and either be very attractive with a great body, or know someone (a female porn actress, director who wants to work with you, a crew member, etc.) who can get you into a movie.

What Qualities Do I Need?

For a girl, apart from a hot body, you need to be able to deliver a hot performance every time. For a guy, you've got to be able to keep wood and "release" on cue.

Also, you'll need the universal qualities that help people in any job—have a good attitude, don't bring your personal problems to work, and be fairly disciplined. No employer likes unreliability.

Does Size Matter?

If you're a guy you don't need a huge cock. At least five inches is good, and a couple more is even better, because the camera needs to see some shaft during penetration.

How Much Money Should I Ask For?

When you're starting off, you may get as little as $100 per scene. Then it's up to you to work hard and climb the porno ladder of success. If you get a reputation for being hot and good to work with, more lucrative offers will come your way.

Generally, girls make more than guys. Girls make between $300 to $2,000 per sex scene, depending on what type of sex is involved. If she's high-profile, like a Playboy Playmate, she'll get top dollar. Guys make about half as much as girls, and their rate is generally the same, regardless of what type of sex they are performing. For a magazine shoot, guys and girls usually get $500 to $800. Once you've done a few magazine shoots, you can raise your movie rate.

Should I Get an Agent?

There are a few good agents and lots of bad ones. Get a friend in the business to recommend a good one. If you get an agent, they can tell you which porno companies to avoid and which ones will treat you well, plus they can negotiate your fee.

Can I Control the Type of Work?

You can decide what you will and won't do—but clearly the more you do, the more money you'll get. You'll have little control over the projects unless you hire your own film crew and photographer. This is expensive, but the upside of running the show yourself is that you get a bigger slice of the royalties, rather than a one-off flat fee.

What about the Internet?

It's a great way to get your wares out to a potentially limitless amount of customers. Get a friend to design a web site, upload your photos and you're in business.

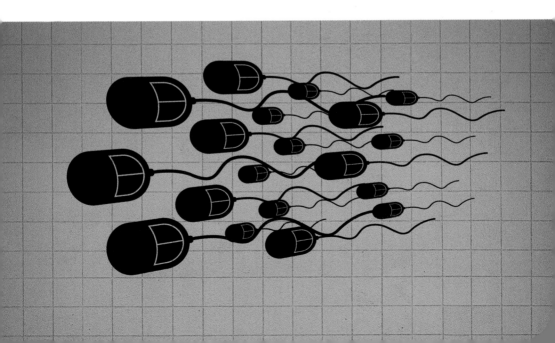

42. Build an Atom Bomb

Whatever you do, don't tell anyone that you are assembling a nuclear device in your garage. A single indiscreet moment down at the bar can land you in big trouble.

Beg, Borrow, and Steal

First obtain several pounds of weapons grade plutonium, or two sub-critical masses of uranium 235. This is the easy part. The stuff is lying around all over the place in the ex-Soviet Union. Take a trip there, and if you can't find any in the chil-

dren's play area of the nearest municipal park, then you will easily be able to bribe a technician in the nuclear industry.

Smuggling it back home is the tricky part. Either bribe a diplomat, who can smuggle it into the country in their lead-lined diplomatic pouch, or hide it in your check-in luggage and hope that the security staff at the airport are having yet another one of their off days.

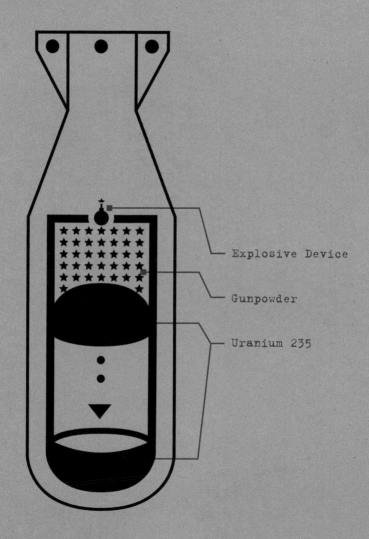

Assembling the Device

Once you get your nuclear fissile material safely home, you need to construct a means of colliding two lumps of the stuff at high speed, to create a nuclear chain reaction. This is the same principle that was used for the Hiroshima bomb—essentially you need to make a double-ended firework. Wear protective clothing, and if at any time you feel nauseous or your hair begins to fall out, seek medical advice immediately.

Get a nine-foot-long piece of metal drain piping and drill several small holes in it at regular intervals. Weld several small lengths of copper pipe onto these holes, then cover the drain pipe in concrete, leaving all the ends (copper and pipe) exposed. The copper pipes act as vent holes, so that the initial explosion doesn't splinter the pipe and send radioactive isotopes in all directions.

Pack each end of the pipe with a generous lump of the nuclear material along with a few pounds of plastic explosive. Rig both sets of explosive up to a detonator and a timer. This can be a simple VCR timer, or better still, a mobile phone set to vibrate. Then you can phone the device from anywhere in the world to detonate the bomb.

You will greatly increase the efficiency of the bomb if you can get your hands on a directional thermal neutron emitter. If not, don't worry about it. Just seal the ends of the pipe by welding metal bungs onto them and then cover with more concrete.

43. Negotiate with Kidnappers

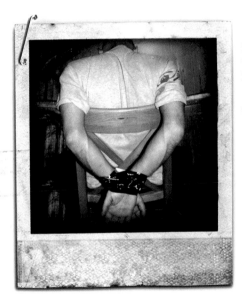

Governments always say: "Don't negotiate with kidnappers. To do so would only invite more." We don't know about you, but most people given $5 million and an Aston Martin DB7 as a getaway vehicle would have to be a workaholic or in a whole lot of debt not to call it a day. Even after you've given 40 percent to your accomplice in the police force, you've still got enough to buy a Pacific island retreat. So, the take-home message is: start the negotiations.

Here are six tips for negotiating the release of your loved ones:

1. If the kidnappers are international terrorists (rather than local crooks) and you live in Japan, Italy, or France, you can open a bottle of champagne now. Your government will have handed over a large wad of unmarked bills before you even knew that your loved one was missing.

2. If you live in the U.S. or U.K., the protocol is more protracted. They will publicly claim no deal, while selling them truckloads of stinger missiles in exchange for drug

money which can then be used to fund anticommunist rebels in Central America.

3. There's no better place to cut your teeth as a negotiator than in Mexico, the kidnapping capital of the world. Official figures show less than 300 kidnappings a year, but the reality is more like ten times that figure. They go unreported because many of the perpetrators are high ranking policemen or ex-policemen. Increasingly, people from middle-income families are becoming the most lucrative victims. So take a vacation to Mexico and you can get in some negotiating practice while you are there.

4. Try to identify the general whereabouts of the hostage. Obviously, if you knew the precise location you could send in your own crack team of privately hired ex-special forces guys, but if you know at least which city or country is holding them you can then make approaches to influential figures around the city or area.

5. Keep the kidnappers on the phone. The more talking they do, the less chance they'll cut off an ear or behead someone. Kidnappers are terrible at multitasking. That's why they always sound so stressed.

44. Bullfight

The Spanish call it corrida de toros; Hemingway called it a grand passion, "the only art in which the artist is in danger of death." Bullfighters need skill, courage, and a Ph.D. in bull psychology.

Bullfighting is a ritual that plays out in specific prearranged steps. First, you and your team enter the arena in a parade, or paseíllo, accompanied by band music. Line up in scar order: the oldest matador goes to the far left, while the newest walks in the middle. You'll be wearing a figurehugging sequined suit called a traje de luces (literally, a suit of lights), and if you're new to the Plaza, you won't be wearing your hat. The bullfight is divided into the following three main parts (tercios):

Tercio De Varas ("Lances Third")

The bull charges into the ring. He is at least four years old, weighs about half a ton, and he's pissed. He is tested for ferocity by you (the matador) and "trained" to follow and attack the cape. The two picadors mounted on horseback impale the bull in its neck with lances. If they throw the lances hard enough they embed themselves so far that the lever effect breaks some of the bull's ribs.

It's your job to execute a series of impressive maneuvers with a very heavy magenta and gold dress cape called a capote. These maneuvers allow you to learn about the bull's behavior, such as whether it charges in straight or curved lines, or whether it has any defects such as eyesight problems or a clubbed foot. You must perform a number of fundamental passes with the cape. The closer you can get the bull to pass by your body, the better. The basic pass, from which all the others spring, is called the "Veronica" in which the cape is drawn over the bull's head while you strike a pose.

Tercio De Banderillas ("Banderillas Third")

Three banderilleros each attempt to plant two brightly-colored barbed sticks (banderillas, literally "little flags") on the bull's flanks causing major loss of blood, and further weakening the animal. You can sit this one out and save your energy for the finale.

Tercio De Muerte ("Death Third")

You re-enter the ring alone with a small red cape in one hand and a thirty-three-inch-long sword in the other. Even though the bull is weakened, he is now at his most dangerous. You execute another set of crowd-pleasing passes, and if you are really daring, you kneel in front of the bull. They love that.

After an impressive pass, look at the crowd, puff out your chest and shout, "Quién es el papá?" (Who's the daddy?). You've got to flaunt it.

Before the kill, dedicate the animal to an individual by handing them your hat (montero), or place your hat on the ground to dedicate the bull to everyone. Kill the bull cleanly and efficiently with style and in a way that exposes you to maximum danger. The act of thrusting the sword is called an estocada. For the best kill, the estocada recibido, allow the bull to charge you while you stand your ground, then thrust the sword between the shoulder blades (a target about the size of your palm). When performed correctly, the bull will expire within minutes. If the crowd really loves you, you'll be rewarded with one or two ears and the tail. Screw it up and you'll be booed and showered with cushions.

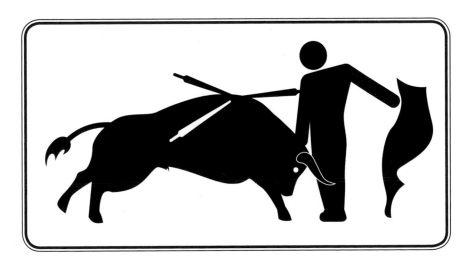

45. Perform Open Heart Surgery

Open heart surgery is often cited as one of the most invasive of all medical procedures, requiring expertise of the highest level for a successful outcome. But hey, it's not brain surgery. Here's how to fix a simple case of stenotic arteriosclerotic coronary artery disease in ten steps, and with no previous medical knowledge (allow between three to four hours for the operation).

1. **Before you begin, familiarize yourself with the anatomy of the heart. In brief, it has a right and left ventricle, and a right and left atrium. The right ventrical pumps oxygen-poor blood into the lungs, and the left ventrical pumps oxygen-rich blood to the rest of the body . . . yawn . . . and swiftly on . . .**

2. **Scrub up. This involves making urbane conversation with your colleagues while washing your hands with yellow soap, and skillfully operating stainless steel taps with your elbows.**

3. **The bit before the operation is called Pre-op. Give the patient a sedative in his arm to keep him calm and to reduce the risk that he'll ask you any tough questions, like "Can**

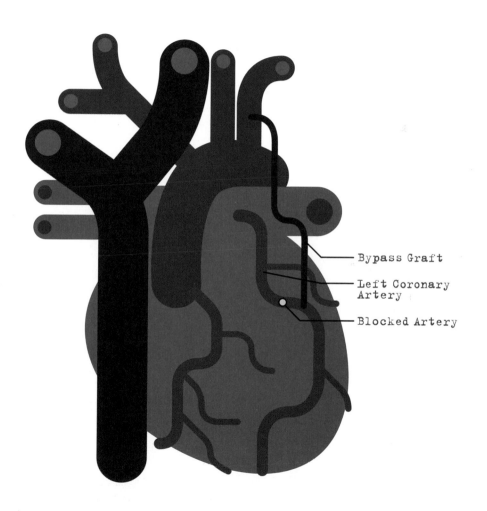

Bypass Graft

Left Coronary
Artery

Blocked Artery

I see some ID?" Shave and scrub the patient's chest area to reduce the risk of infection. Finally, make sure you have an anesthesiologist (who puts the patient to sleep) and a perfusionist (who is responsible for the oxygenation of the blood). Basically, they keep the patient alive while you get to do all the fun stuff.

4. Once the patient is unconscious, cut open the leg and grab a piece of the saphenous vein. You'll need this later to create the bypass.

5. Make an incision down the center of the patient's chest, then crank open the breastbone with a sternal retractor.

6. Slice down the middle of the pericardium, the membranous sac which contains the heart.

7. Get one of the nurses to mop your brow.

8. Make two slits in the coronary artery wall above and below the blockage, then carefully sew the leg vessel graft onto the coronary artery using very fine synthetic sutures. Repeat steps 7 and 8, depending on how many grafts are required.

9. Attach temporary pacemaker wires to the right and left atrium; this will be used during the patient's recovery to correct any irregular heartbeats.

10. Insert a chest drain to remove excess fluid, stitch up the chest, and then send out for pizza. The patient should remain in the intensive care unit (ICU) for one to two days, then in the hospital for another five days for monitoring.

46. Count Cards at a Casino

Card counting is the only way you can statistically improve your chances of winning at the blackjack table, but then only by a few percent. In the film Rain Man, Dustin Hoffman's character memorizes an eight deck shoe, but in real life, you don't have to be an autistic savant with a photographic memory to use a card counting system, of which there are hundreds, but we will discuss the most common.

— Golden Rule: Don't Get Caught. —

Counting cards isn't illegal, so long as you use your brain and not an electronic device. However, that doesn't mean that a casino will tolerate you if they suspect you of counting. Many casinos are private property, so they can throw you out without giving a reason and charge you with trespassing if you return. In some joints, the dealers count too, and shuffle the pack when the odds swing in your favor. Many casinos use eight deck shoes and prohibit mid-shoe entry, which means that you can't just join when the decks are looking good.

When you play blackjack, certain cards favor the dealer and other cards favor the player. Very simply, the more high cards left in the shoe, the better the player's chances of winning, because a dealer must hit if he has less than 17. But you don't have to remember every single card that has been played; you just need to keep a running tally of hi versus lo cards.

THE HI/LO SYSTEM

Ace	2	3	4	5	6	7	8	9	10	Jack	Queen	King
-1	+1	+1	+1	+1	+1	0	0	0	-1	-1	-1	-1

As each card is dealt, add or subtract 1 from your running total. The higher the total, the better your odds and the more you bet; zero means it's 50-50; and a negative number means the dealer has the advantage.

So, if the deal is A, 8, 5, 2, 9, K, J, then the running total will be -1, -1, 0, +1, +1, 0, -1. However, you also have to divide the running total by the number of decks of cards still in the shoe to get a true count.

BET SPREAD

This means betting high when your chances are good and low when they are not. For instance, you may bet $80 on good hands and $10 on low. However, in light of the golden rule, if you make the bet spread (the difference between your big and small bets) too obvious (i.e., more than 8 to 1), you may get invited to a backroom beating.

USE THIS TABLE AS A ROUGH BET SPREAD GUIDE:

True Count	Betting Units
+1	1
+2 or +3	2
+4 or +5	3
+6 or +7	4
+8 or +9	5

   Be patient and try to look like a tourist or a loser gambler bum rather than a card-counting newbie. Counting cards will not make you a millionaire overnight. The glory days of card counting are long gone anyway, because the casinos have made the game more difficult to beat by increasing the number of decks, limiting bet spreads, and capping bets. You could make more money by getting yourself an evening job in a 7-Eleven or pumping gas.

47. Screw Up Someone's Car

There are too many cars on the road, so screwing over an enemy's vehicle is good for you and the environment. Fortunately, there are lots of subtle and not-so-subtle ways to mess with their engine without having to take a baseball bat to the paintwork, which is time consuming and wakes up the neighbors. Here are a few quieter solutions and a sweet myth exploded.

Sugar in the Gas Tank

We've all heard of this one. The sugar is supposed to dissolve in the gas and then caramelize once it reaches the pistons. The trouble is, sugar isn't soluble in gas, so all it really does is clog up the fuel filter and starve the engine of air. It will definitely cause problems, but is unlikely to total the engine. A better solution is to pour diesel into the tank of a gasoline car. This will wreck the engine. Pouring regular gas into a diesel engine won't destroy it, but will require the tank to be drained, which should cost at least $150.

Oil Trouble

Drain the oil from the oil pan. The car will seize up within minutes and destroy the engine. However, unless you cut the wires leading to the gauges, a warning light will come on to say there's no oil. So replace the oil with very thin oil, like two-cycle oil. This will cause engine damage without tripping the oil light. Alternatively, leave the oil intact but replace the oil drain plug with a cork. Once the car has warmed up, the crankcase pressure will blow the cork and oil out very quickly, causing lots of damage before the warning light comes on.

Cavity Wall Filler

Drill a small hole in the window and pump in a large can of expanding foam filler which grows to thirty times the dispensed amount and hardens within minutes.

Styrene Solution

Pouring a pint of styrene (autobody resin) in the crankcase will make the engine lock up tight within a hundred miles.

Fruit and Vegetables

Make sure your victim gets at least one of his five portions of fruits and veggies—up his exhaust pipe. Ram it in hard with a broom handle and a mechanic will have to strip down half the engine before he finds the fault.

Ricer Self-Destruction

If your victim is a ricer (a dumb ass who makes unnecessary modifications to their—most often imported Japanese—car to make it look like it goes faster), then the easiest way to screw up his car is to give him $1,000 and let him destroy it himself with unnecessary performance mods. Next time you see him, he'll have a ten-inch exhaust tip, incorrect badging, seat harnesses, offset tape stripes, a single wiper conversion, and an over-sized fiberglass bodykit. One speed bump and he'll crash into a tree.

If none of the above appeals to you, steal the car, drive it to an upper-class suburb, and set it on fire.

48. Climb the Pyramids

The three great pyramids of Giza are located on the Giza Plateau a few miles southwest of Cairo, in Egypt. Climbing them is illegal, since it damages the stones and the 51 degree incline is very steep; many people have been killed in the attempt.

An Irresistible Challenge

When the pyramids were built they were surfaced with highly polished white limestone casing stones to create a dazzling smooth surface. Over the centuries, most of these stones have been either eroded or stolen to expose the stair-like structure that now beckons us to climb.

Bribe the Guards

A daytime ascent is not suggested because you would simply be caught and arrested by the guards. You must sneak into the compound under the cover of darkness, at about 3 A.M.. Guards with dogs still patrol the perimeter of the complex, but if caught you may be able to bribe them.

Make your way to the north face of the pyramids, which are in relative darkness (the sides that face Cairo are illuminated with spotlights). Menkaure is the smallest and easiest pyramid to climb and it is also the furthest away from the entrance, but at 204 feet it is less than half the height of the others. You won't be able to reach the very top of the middle pyramid, Khafre, because it still has casing stones at the summit, but Khufu, the real challenge, is there for the taking.

Pyramid of Khufu

Khufu is the oldest and tallest of the pyramids and the only surviving member of the Seven Wonders of the Ancient World. It was completed in 2560 B.C. and remained the tallest manmade structure in the world for more than 3,800 years (until the construction of the spire of Lincoln Cathedral in Great Britain in 1300 A.D.). It was 480 feet high, but with erosion it now stands 455 feet high. The record ascent and descent time was achieved by an Egyptian guide who could climb up and down in less than seven minutes. He used to perform this feat for visiting dignitaries at the command of President Nasser.

Enjoy the View

When you reach the summit, you will enjoy a spectacular view of Cairo and the desert, and can ponder about the people who have stood at the same vantage point. In 1798, just before the Battle of Giza, Napoleon Bonaparte observed, "From atop these pyramids, forty centuries look down upon you." Soak it up—you will probably fall and break your neck during the treacherous descent.

THE MOST FORBIDDEN KNOWLEDGE

49. Find the Ark of the Covenant

The Ark of the Covenant is the wooden box that housed Aaron's rod, some *manna* (the miracle food which kept the Israelites alive before matza balls were invented), and the sacred Tablets of Stone which Moses brought down from Mount Sinai, bearing the Ten Commandments.

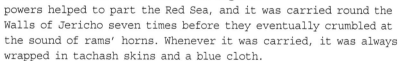

Magic Box

The Ark was a powerful talisman for the Israelites, who carried it around with them in the wilderness, and into battle, born by Levite priests, 2,000 cubits (about half a mile) in front of them. Its magical powers helped to part the Red Sea, and it was carried round the Walls of Jericho seven times before they eventually crumbled at the sound of rams' horns. Whenever it was carried, it was always wrapped in tachash skins and a blue cloth.

Where Did You Last See It?

As your mother will tell you, the best way to find something is to work out when it was last seen, which in the case of the Ark, was 2,500 years ago. We know that it was housed in the First Temple by Solomon around 950 B.C. Later it is mentioned in the Old Testament in II Chronicles 35:3, when King Josiah (who ruled in the seventh century B.C.) instructed the Levites: "Put the holy ark in the house which Solomon the son of David, king of Israel, built; you need no longer carry it upon your shoulders." Scholars don't know whether the Levites followed his instructions, although if they'd been carrying it around for 350 years, they must have been glad to rest.

Possible Hiding Places

1. Nebuchadnezzar destroyed the Temple in 586 B.C., so if the Ark was there it could also have been destroyed or taken to Babylon (although it isn't mentioned in the book of Jeremiah with all the other spoil). Babylon is in present-day Iraq about fifty-five miles south of Baghdad. Good luck with that one.

2. Jeremiah hid it on Mount Nebo shortly before the Babylonian attack, or possibly one of the many caves in the area where the Dead Sea Scrolls were found.

3. According to biblical scholar Leen Ritmeyer, there's a rectangular hollow carved out in the bedrock of the Muslim Dome of the Rock Shrine in Jerusalem, with exactly the same dimensions as the Ark. He believes this is the site of the Second Temple. The hollow is empty, which indicates that the Ark could well be in Ritmeyer's garage. However, there is also a complex system of secret chambers underneath the Shrine, but the Supreme Muslim Council, the Wakf, hasn't allowed any excavations on the site and many scholars believe that the Ark was never placed in the Second Temple at all.

4. Another candidate is the Church of St. Mary of Zion in Axum, Ethiopia. The Ethiopian Orthodox Church claims to have possessed the Ark, of the Covenant since the early Middle Ages. It is guarded by a large group of bouncer monks with instructions to kill all intruders who attempt to enter the Holy of Holies where the Ark is kept. Only one monk is allowed access to the Ark, and, once appointed, he spends the rest of his life in the Holy of Holies— never to be allowed out again. Apply for the position in writing, enclosing a stamped addressed envelope with your application.

Church of St. Mary of Zion in Axum

50. Hunt a Yeti in the Himalayas

The Himalayas are the highest range of mountains in the world. The "roof of the world" is home to Mount Everest, and the yeti, which most people agree is a giant hairy bipedal ape. The Nepalese call it *Ban-manche* (forest man) and *Kangchen-junga rachyyas* (Kangchenjunga's demon). If you want to find the yeti, wrap up warm and start climbing.

Dhaulagiri

The hottest recent yeti sightings have been on the slopes of Dhaulagiri, the world's fifth highest mountain, in western Nepal. Japan's most famous yeti-hunter, Yoshiteru Takahashi claims to have found a yeti cave here, but his camera froze before he could take a picture. However, on subsequent expeditions to the area, he has photographed footprints using nine motion-sensitive cameras.

Friend or Foe

In most encounters the yeti has run away, so it would probably flee, unless it was cornered, or very hungry. Run-ins with the yeti have been both hostile and friendly. A Sherpa girl was dragged off by the yeti, who released her after she screamed, and then killed two of her yaks; by contrast, in 1938, Captain d'Auvergue, the curator of the Victoria Memorial in Calcutta, India, reported that he was cared for by a nine-foot-tall yeti after becoming snowblind.

Ape with Altitude

Most sightings of the yeti have occurred at altitudes between 15,000 and 20,000 feet. Sightings have been reported since the early nineteenth century, but the first reliable one took place in 1925. Greek photographer N. A. Tombazi spotted one about three hundred yards away at an altitude of 15,000 feet. He described a "figure in outline . . . exactly like a human being" that "showed up dark against the snow." The creature disappeared, but Tombazi discovered fifteen footprints in the snow measuring seven inches by four, with five toes.

In 1951, footprints eighteen inches long and thirteen inches wide were photographed on the southwestern slopes of the Menlung Glacier, between Tibet and Nepal at an altitude of 20,000 feet. Your best chances of a sighting are at these high altitudes, where the landscape is most remote and undisturbed by people. Avoid Everest, as there are too many lunatics trying to kill themselves there and that will scare the yeti away. As put by Edmund Hillary, the first man to conquer Everest: "There is precious little in civilization to appeal to a yeti."

51. Claim Political Asylum

If you don't want your vacation to end and you can't face your responsibilities back home, claiming asylum is a great way to stay at the party. The United Nations 1951 Convention Relating to the Status of Refugees and the 1967 Protocol Relating to the Status of Refugees provides the legislation that applies to asylum.

In order to claim asylum successfully, you must prove that you are unable to return to your home country, or your main country of residence if you are stateless because you fear persecution there under protected grounds, which include race, nationality, politics, religion, sexuality, and membership and/or participation in any particular social group or social activities.

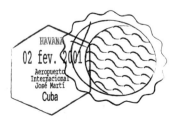

HAVANA
02 fev. 2001
Aeropuerto
Internacional
José Martí
Cuba

United Kingdom

The UK has a soft spot for asylum seekers, and receives the largest number of applications. This means that there's a huge backlog in processing, so even if your request is unsuccessful, in the meantime you'll be able to spend so many years in the country that you will be able to claim de facto citizenship and squatter's rights when the Queen tries to throw you out. You'll receive an allowance of about £40 a week, most of which is Fortnum & Mason food vouchers. After six months you can apply for the right to work, and you'll be given accommodation if you can prove you're destitute. Pray you get a hostel rather than a detention center.

Pros: the UK has the best justice system in the world, despite the Guildford Four, the Birmingham Six, the Bridgwater Four, and the M25 Three.

Cons: the beer is warm, but Brits don't care because they spend most of the time dumping it on their heads, and they can't watch a soccer match without throwing seats.

Germany

Recently knocked off the top asylum spot by the UK, the pocket money isn't great (about 50 euro per week), you'll be housed in a reception center, and you won't have the right to work until your applications has been processed.

Pros: they are just like most of the folks back home: loud, fat, and carnivorous, except that they can speak better English.

Cons: their male tennis players have transparent eyebrows, all the stores close for lunch, and it takes seven minutes to pour a half pint of beer.

France

There's a six-month waiting list for housing in an overcrowded reception center, and you need to apply for a temporary residence permit from the local authorities, for which there is also a six-month wait. Your allowance is four pounds of Camembert and two bottles of Vin de Table per day.

Pros: they have the most corrupt Olympic ice-skating judges in the world, and French women braid their underarm hair.

Cons: they think Jerry Lewis is a comic genius, per capita they buy the least soap and toothbrushes of any European country, and drugs are so prevalent in national sports that it is not uncommon for cyclists' heads to explode during the Alpine stages of the Tour de France.

52. Play with Booze and Fire

Pure alcohol burns so well that we can use it as an alternative fuel to gasoline for cars. This means you can have all sorts of fun with the less pure stuff that you can find in any well-stocked bar.

Get Proof

To get a decent flame from a drink, it should be at least 100 proof (50% alcohol). The higher the alcohol content, the easier it is for a liquid to burn. Those who regularly mess around with drinks and lighters usually employ Everclear (190 proof) or Barcardi 151 (151 proof).

Because of their high alcohol content, these drinks normally come mixed with something else to make them more palatable. When working with fire, though, it's best to stick to plain liquor straight up.

Play with Fire

Next, find yourself a decent source of fire. You can use a lighter, but turning the thing upside-down to get the flame nearer to the booze can cause you to set your thumb on fire. Instead, get one of those long-tipped butane lighters used for lighting barbecue grills. In a pinch, a match works well too, as long as you work quickly. Just don't forget to put the match out when you're done with it.

Favorite Flames

The most popular mixture of booze and fire is the flaming shot. To pull this off:

1. **Get a high-proof shot.**

2. **Light it.**

3. **Slam it.**

4. **Close your mouth.**

If you do this right, the fire will burn out shortly after entering your mouth, as closing your mouth suffocates the blaze. Of course, if you blow it, just remember those famous words every kid learns during the fire safety classes at school. "Stop, drop, and roll."

And Liberty for All

The Statue of Liberty is a fun variant on the standard flaming shot. To handle this one:

1. Get a shot.

2. Dip your finger in it.

3. Have a friend light your finger.

4. Hold your finger up like a torch as you slam back the shot.

5. Stick your finger in your mouth and close it to extinguish the flame.

53. Knock Someone Out

You see it on every cheesy detective show in the world. The PI walks into a room and a shadowy figure steps up and pistol whips him from behind. The detective slumps over unconscious but otherwise unharmed. He wakes up a short time later with blood all over the place and a stillhot pistol in his hand. He's been framed for a murder and it all goes downhill from there.

Reality Check

In real life, it doesn't work this way. When someone loses consciousness from a blow, it almost always means he's sustained a serious concussion. When the victim wakes up, he will be hurt and disoriented and may vomit.

That's not the worst-case scenario. A hit that can knock someone out might kill them instead. It's easy to see how a blow to the skull might crack it wide open or how a severe concussion could lead to bleeding in the brain.

In other words, don't try this at home.

Hit Fast and Hard

If you need to knock someone out, there are two simple ways to do it: punching or choking. Again, either can be lethal, so attempt these only as a last resort. It's often enough to hit someone hard and then run away while they're hurting. Knocking them out isn't necessary.

Knock-Out Punch

Swing your fist hard and fast straight at the center of your target's jaw. Aim right through him rather than trying to jab. With a solid enough hit, you will slam his head back fast enough to rattle his brain, which is what you're hoping to do. You might break your hand doing this, but if you're that desperate it may be a small price to pay.

The Dim Mak school of martial arts—which focuses on the delivery of strikes to bundles of nerves in the victim's body—prescribes striking your foe in the temple with a shaped fist. This, again, can be lethal.

Choke-Out

On either side of the throat, there's a carotid artery. You can feel your pulse in it with your bare fingers. Pressure on these cuts off circulation of blood to the brain, which eventually causes the victim to pass out. This doesn't carry the risk of head trauma, but it can kill if you keep the pressure up for too long. Again, it's better to hit and run.

54. Amputate a Limb

It's one of the most horrific things to think about—losing a part of your own body—but it's better to cut loose a piece if it means a chance to save your life. Some people have even managed to do this to themselves when necessary.

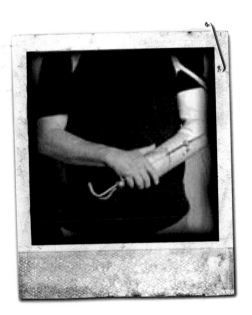

This is of course a last resort, often only employed if a part of the body is trapped and unable to be freed. Perhaps it's caught in a burning thresher or crushed under a boulder, leaving the victim no other way to get free and to help. However, an impromptu amputation in the field is likely to kill you too. Only try this if the alternative is clearly death.

Here's how to do it.

Make a Tourniquet

If you haven't already done so, make a tourniquet and place it around the limb that's about to be lost. This will help deaden the pain of the cutting and also prevent you from bleeding out after the loss of the limb. Place the tourniquet as far down the limb as you can manage so that you can save as much flesh as possible.

Use a Sharp Knife

The sharper the blade you can find, the better. Dull knives hurt more and can slip during the procedure.

Find a Space in the Bones— or Make One

The hardest part of any amputation is getting through the bone. If you have a saw handy, you may be able to cut right through the bone. Otherwise, you may be forced to break it. Place the bone on something firm and use your weight as leverage to snap it.

If this isn't possible, look for the nearest joint to the damaged area. It's far easier to cut through cartilage and tendons than through solid bone.

Get Medical Help

Once you're free, administer what first aid you can to stop the bleeding and help with the shock. Then get proper medical attention right away. With luck, you'll live.

55. Practice Gun Fu

If you've watched too many John Woo movies, you know that all true gunsels hold their pistols sideways and out away from their bodies as they empty clip after clip into their foes. It's ridiculous, and it makes it hard to hit anything you think you might be aiming at, but it looks cool. So, if style means more to you than actually hitting anything with a bullet, then gun fu is for you.

Shoot Wild but Pretty

Use semi-automatic pistols or at least learn how to pull that trigger fast. Gun fu practitioners buy bullets in bulk and throw them around like a flower girl tosses petals.

It doesn't matter if you hit your target, at least not right away. You can chase them down with bullets, herd them into the place you want them to be, and then administer a balletic coup de grace that will make your victim appreciate how beautifully you stole his final breath.

Use as Many Guns as You Can

Put a machine-pistol in each hand, an assault rifle slung across your back, and a sawed-off shotgun on your hip. Use them in tandem and individually in any order you can manage. Bonus points for establishing some kind of beat. Double that if you can dance to it.

Ammo Like Water

Run through enough ammunition that you'll need to carry your spare clips in a cart you pull behind you—between scenes in the movie that is your life, of course. In the heat of battle, drop magazines out of your weapons one-handed, letting them fall to the ground. Then flip spare clips out of your sleeves and straight into the guns once again.

Cock your weapons with one hand, especially shotguns. That way you can fill both of your fists with them at once.

Die a Blood Death

Unless you're the hero of this flick, be prepared to die by the weapon of your choice. You should have spent all that practice time playing mah jong instead for all the good it will do you.

56. Get Hit by a Car and Survive

Do yourself a favor and do like your momma taught you. Look both ways before you cross the street, and don't play in traffic. You'll live a lot longer that way.

If you still find yourself on the wrong side of a fast-moving grill, let's hope the words in this chapter find enough time to flash through your head before you die. Then you can at least tell St. Peter you gave it a shot.

Watch the Road

If you see the car coming, you may have a chance. Figure out which way it's going and dive in the other direction. Just try not to dive into more traffic if you can.

Seek Cover

If this is no accident—if someone's actually trying to hit you with the car—then dive behind something solid. All but the most determined hit-and-run artists won't purposely destroy their car trying to get at you. After all, if they crack up the car, they blow that ever-important "run" part of their plan.

Up and Over

If you cannot get away from the car, for whatever reason, then jump up. Get as high as you can, and pull your legs up after you. If you're channeling Michael Jordan—or facing a really short car—you might even be able to clear the top of the vehicle and let it pass under. Chances are, though, that you'll get at least clipped instead.

Still, bouncing off the top of a car beats having it run over you any day.

Roll with It

Once you've been hit, pull yourself into a ball and cover up your head with your arms if you can. The impact is likely to send you flying, and the better your landing, the better your chance of surviving. If you flail about trying to flap away through the air, you're only going to break a limb or—worse—your neck.

57. Make a Shiv

A shiv is a homemade knife made from whatever you happen to have handy. In most cases, it's far simpler to go to your nearest store and just buy a knife, but when that's not an option—like, say, if you're in prison—then here's what you do.

Find Something Long and Hard

And get your mind out of the gutter. You'll have enough problems with that sort of thing in jail.

Find something hard that fits well in your hand. A piece of metal is perfect, but wood or plastic will do if it's hard enough. Even a longish bit of bone from a meal will work.

The more the item is shaped like a knife, the better. Knives have been around for thousands of years, and they're made the way they are for a reason.

Sharpen the end of this thing. It might be a metal strut from a bed frame, the metal shank from a boot, or even a spoon, but it's no good to you if it's dull. Rub it methodically against something rough, like cement, until it's sharp. Try to work on both sides equally and to make the blade that you're forming smooth. This makes it easier to maintain than something jagged.

Find Something Sharp

If you can't find something long to sharpen, then find something sharp and make it long. If you have a piece of glass or a razor blade, that's a fine start. It's hard to use something like that effectively, though, without cutting yourself as well, so you need to fashion a handle.

Fastening the sharp bit to a stick or even a toothbrush can work well. To make it stay put, you can even try driving the sharp point straight through the makeshift handle. Then bind it up with a bit of string or cloth to help keep it from falling apart in the middle of a fight.

If you can't find anything else, wrap a piece of cloth around one end of the sharp thing. This isn't the best solution, as something truly sharp will cut through the cloth eventually too, but it should let you get in a couple good stabs before that happens.

58. Kite Checks

Sometimes you just need a little extra cash to tide you over. Or maybe you have a hot tip about a no-fail horse or stock. If you're strapped enough to try something illegal, you might consider kiting checks. Here's how it works.

What You Need

1. Two bank accounts.

2. Checks for each.

How You Do it

1. Write a check to yourself from one bank account (the First National Bank) and deposit it in your other bank account (the Second National Bank). This normally takes a day to clear from the other bank, but the deposit will show up immediately in your Second National Bank account, covering any other checks that might otherwise bounce.

2. The next business day, write a check to yourself from the Second National Bank and deposit it in your First National Bank account. This should cover the check you wrote the previous day. Again, it will take a day for the transfer to catch up with you.

3. Rinse and repeat until:

    a. You come up with enough money to legitimately cover the shortfall; or

    b. You get caught.

Penalties

Check kiting is fraud and can carry stiff penalties. Doing so for small amounts might only be a misdemeanor (which is still serious), but larger amounts can constitute felony. The maximum penalty is a million-dollar fine and thirty years in jail.

59. Avoid Bounty Hunters

If you have a bounty hunter on your tail, you're in serious trouble. It usually means you're a fugitive from the law, and there's a substantial price on your head. While it's hard enough having the law after you, bounty hunters are often more willing to bend the rules to capture you. After all, they're not worried about getting a conviction; they just want to bring you in.

Here are ten tips to keep them off your ass.

1. Leave your clothes behind and buy a new set that looks nothing like what you usually wear.

2. If you have facial hair, shave it. If you don't (and you're a man), grow it.

3. Dye your hair a different color, or shave it off altogether.

4. If you wear glasses, get contacts. If you don't wear glasses, then start.

5. Lose some weight or put some on.

6. Credit and debit cards leave a trail that's easy to follow. Clean out your bank accounts and (if you don't care about credit problems) max out the cash advances on your credit cards, and leave town.

7. Toss out your cell phone. It contains a GPS function that can be used to track your location. If you must have a phone, pick up a pay-as-you-go version and then toss it out when you use up the minutes.

8. Phone people you know only when you must. Communication by e-mail is harder to follow, although it can sometimes be traced to your general location. You might even consider communicating via Skype or over an online gaming service (like Xbox Live or *World of Warcraft*) instead.

9. If you're well-known in a particular field, avoid it.

10. Avoid public events or any position that might get your picture in the paper or on the evening news

60. Get Rid of a Body

How you wound up with a body is not important. You're just concerned about getting rid of it. There are dozens of ways you can try. Here are ten.

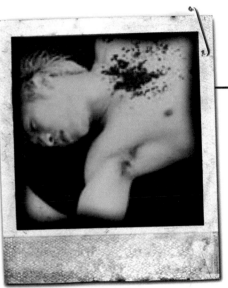

1. Sell it to a mad scientist for medical experiments.

2. Chain cement blocks to it and drop it in a large body of water.

3. Find an incinerator. If you can get access to one used to cremate bodies, all the better. Use it.

4. Bury it in the desert. If you're near Las Vegas, take care you don't dig someone else up while you're at it.

5. Break open *How to Cook Everything*. Get cooking.

6. Toss it into an active volcano.

7. Bury it in your cellar.

8. Stuff it inside a hide-a-bed couch and put it on the curb.

9. Ship it to China via ocean freighter.

10. Just walk away. Okay, run.

61. Chemically Enhance Your Athletic Performance

Not a season seems to go by these days without one professional athlete or another being embroiled in a scandal over one kind of performance-enhancing drug or another. Here are some of the things they take, and why.

1. Anabolic steroids. The stuff you use is synthetic testosterone, which helps build muscle fast. It also gives you zits, destroys your liver, shrinks your balls, drives you bald, and makes you more aggressive and prone to depression.

2. Androstendione. This hormone, known as andro, supposedly pushes your body to make more testosterone. Recent studies, though, show that it doesn't work. However, it still has horrible side-effects like anabolic steroids and can screw around with your blood cholesterol to boot.

3. Creatine. This is a natural compound that you can get from eating meat or fish—or in pill form. It gives a short-term boost to your muscles, although it does nothing for endurance. However, it can cause cramps, vomiting, diarrhea, and harm your heart, kidneys, and liver. It is legal to use, but because the FDA doesn't regulate it, it's hard to know if you're getting the right stuff.

4. Stimulants. Things like caffeine and speed or even meth can make you as twitchy-fast as a puppy on crack. However, they can also make you nervous and grouchy, which is no good during a game. Also, they can cause heart troubles, high blood pressure, convulsions, hallucinations, and even bleeding in the brain.

5. Diuretics. These make you pee. A lot. If you need to drop into a lower weight class, that might be just what you want. Also, it can dilute your urine, which might make it easier to pass when you're tested for any of the other substances. However (you knew it was coming again, didn't you?), they can also cause cramps, weariness, and heart irregularities, among other problems.

62. Saw a Woman in Half

There are many ways of sawing a woman in half. Some magicians use chainsaws, others use rotary saws. In this explanation, all you need is a large handsaw and a person-sized box made of a soft wood that is easy to cut through. Don't make the box too thick or you'll run out of energy before you're finished.

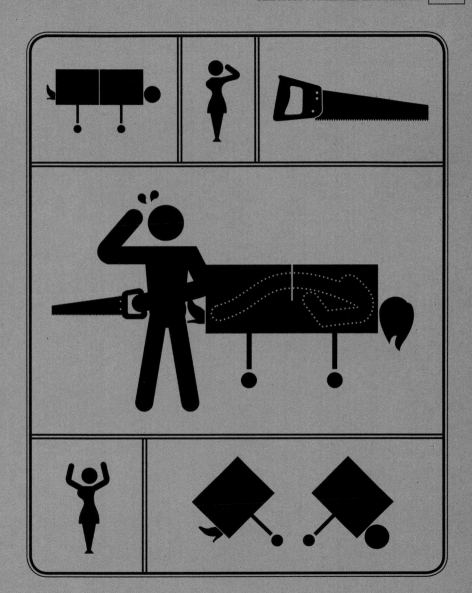

1. Your assistant steps into the empty crate and lies down on her back.

2. You place the lid on top and nail it down.

3. Saw through the middle of the crate until you reach about halfway (you could replace the wood in the center of the crate with strips of insulation board to make it easier to saw through).

4. Stop and pull the saw out and make a big deal of how tired you are and that you need to take a rest.

5. Place the saw back into the groove from the side (not from the top). The reason for this is that while you were "resting," your assistant has arched her back, so that when you replace the saw it is now underneath her body (she can help to guide the saw).

6. Keep sawing until you reach the bottom of the box. It will fall open to reveal an intact assistant.

7. If you are doing this on the street, now is the time to pass around the hat. Collect as much money as you can, then split before the crowd figures out how easily you've tricked them.

63. Play Russian Roulette

Russian roulette is thought to have been invented by depressive Tsarist officers in the Russian army around 1917. On a wet afternoon when daytime television fails to hold your attention and you are beginning to question your own existence, playing a few rounds can be quite a blast.

Health Warning

Do not under any circumstances use a semiautomatic pistol. If there is a single round in the magazine, there is a 100 percent chance that it will fire. Even if the magazine is removed, there may still be one bullet in the barrel (on February 28, 2000, a nineteen-year-old man from Houston, Texas, made this mistake, and used a .45-caliber semiautomatic pistol for Russian roulette, unaware that his chances of survival were zero).

Repeat-Spin Sudden Death

The referee places a round in one of the six chambers of a revolver and spins the cylinder quickly. While it is still spinning, he slaps it sharply back into the body of the gun. If the cylinder is spun inside the body of the gun, the gun should be pointed downwards, otherwise the weight of the bullet tends to make the cylinder come to rest with the bullet toward the bottom, increasing the odds that when the trigger is pulled the hammer will be in contact with an empty chamber (or if you're using a gun like a Mateba Autorevolver, which fires the round in the lower position, you'll greatly increase your risk of being killed).

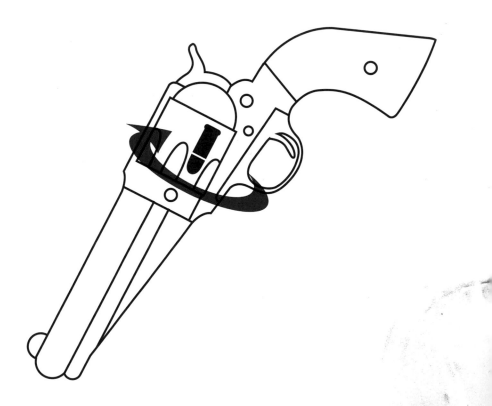

The air should be thick with cigar smoke and crystal meth, and to increase the tension the onlookers will be screaming at each other while waving their wads of cash.

The first player places the gun to his forehead and pulls the trigger. He has just under a 17 percent chance of being killed, which is poor odds compared to most regulated wagering games, especially considering that lives are at risk (for example, in casino craps games, the house pays out 98 percent of what it takes).

The referee spins the cylinder again and hands the gun to the second player who puts it to his forehead and pulls the trigger. The game continues until someone blows their brains out.

Single-Spin Sudden Death

In this variation, there are six players and the cylinder is spun only once, at the beginning. The odds of the first player being killed are 6 to 1. However, if the first four players survive, the odds of player five being killed becomes 2 to 1. If he survives, player six is guaranteed to die, either by his own hand, or shot by incensed bystanders when he tries to escape. However, at the start of the game, the sixth player has the greatest odds of surviving, so pick this position if you are given a choice.

64. Beat a Lie Detector Test

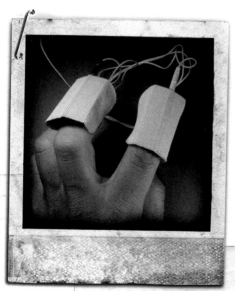

The best way to beat the test is to refuse to take one. Even if your employer demands it, it is illegal for them to sack you if you refuse. If your polygraph is for a criminal investigation, your refusal is generally inadmissible in court. However, with a potential employer, you have no choice but to get hooked up to a polygraph if you want the job. In this case, your best weapon is the knowledge that these tests are fallible.

An Inexact Science

Former FBI Supervisory Special Agent Dr. Drew C. Richardson has described polygraph screening as "completely without any theoretical foundation" and, he says, "has absolutely no validity . . . the diagnostic value of this type of testing is no more than that of astrology or tea-leaf reading." In other words, polygraphs frequently produce incorrect results.

How the Test Works

The examiner will ask you three types of question: irrelevant, relevant, and control. An example of an irrelevant question is "What is your name?" or "What color is your shirt?" A relevant question pertains to the issue in question: "Did you steal the money?" or "Have you ever taken illicit drugs?" These questions will elicit an emotional response, such as raised blood pressure, pulse, sweat response, and breathing, all of which are measured by the polygraph machine. This response will be compared to readings taken when you answer the control questions. These will induce a mild emotional response but aren't relevant to the investigation, such as "Have you ever lied to your parents?" or "Have you broken the speed limit this week?"

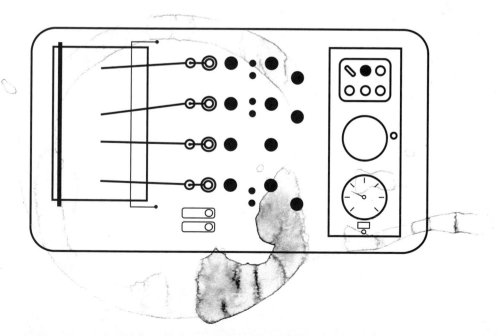

Don't Be Dominated by the Examiner

The average polygraph test lasts about three hours. The longest part is the pretest interview, during which many people give away important information because they are off their guard. During this period, the examiner will try to convince you that the polygraph cannot be beaten and will try to induce feelings of guilt. Don't succumb to his tricks.

How to Fake Your Responses

You need to ensure that the deviation from normal during your responses to control questions is greater than during the relevant questions. There are several ways to do this:

Bite your tongue hard to trigger a pain response.

Do math in your head, such as counting backwards in threes from a hundred.

Think of something that makes you frightened.

Alter your breathing rate.

Tense your sphincter muscle.

Never Make a Relevant Admission

This may seem obvious, but remember that the machine cannot detect lying, only your physiological responses, so don't admit to anything. The examiner can only work with what you tell him.

65. Commit Identity Fraud

Are your bills mounting up? Are collectors and loan sharks constantly knocking on your door? Maybe you just want to run up debts on someone else's credit cards.

Identity Change: Paper Tripping

Although this method is not without its risks, it is the oldest system of identity change in existence. Simply wander around a large cemetery until you find the gravestone of a child who was born around the same time as you, but who died in infancy, without a Social Security number, bank account, or other forms of I.D. Make sure the child is of the same gender and race as you, then assume the identity of the dead infant. Use the information on the gravestone to obtain a copy of the birth certificate, which you can use to get other vital items of identification. State and local registrars are required by law to make birth and death records public, so you can easily access physical records at government offices.

The danger of this method is that there's no guarantee that the grave you choose hasn't already been visited by someone else with the same idea, often a member of the criminal fraternity. This means that your new identity could easily make you one of the FBI's ten most wanted.

– Identity Fraud Phishing Scam –

Send off thousands of emails at random saying that a major U.S. bank has gone bankrupt. On the email, include a link to an official-looking website that you have already set up. Your email advises that customers are starting to panic, so in response clients are advised to access their accounts to check that they are still in credit. Your website will contain a Trojan virus that captures user details for accessing their account, so that you can log in as them and steal money from their account. Launder the money by making false employment offers promising a significant income in a very short time, for allowing you to transfer a large sum into victim's accounts, which they must then transfer to (offshore) accounts that you have set up.

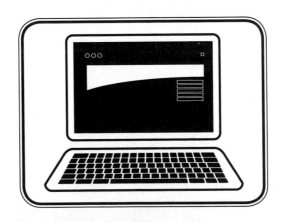

66. Counterfeit Money

You don't need anyone to point out the benefits of forging your own money over working in a soulless job for forty years. Before the arrival of desktop publishing, counterfeiting used to be an expensive operation, but now anyone can buy a PC, a scanner, and a high-end inkjet laser printer and become a paper millionaire without leaving their bedroom.

1. Put a $50 bill on your scanner and scan it at the highest resolution (at least 2,400 dpi). The bill has several security features, some of which can be overcome with the scanner: the entire bill is imprinted with a hexagonal pattern of faint and fine lines, as well as intricate etched details, all of which can be picked up in a high-resolution scan. The hard parts are finding the correct paper and the printing process. If you use a high-quality inkjet printer, the hexagons and intricate detailing will be preserved and will look convincing to the naked eye, even if they do not stand up to scrutiny under a magnifying glass.

2. Ordinary paper is made out of wood pulp. Counterfeit bills that have been printed on ordinary paper not only feel thicker and easily tear, they can be easily detected using a counterfeit pen which contains iodine (which changes color on contact with the cellulose in the paper). Real bills are printed on special "rag" paper that is made from cotton and linen fibers, which also contains minute red and blue silk threads. Obtain a supply of fine red and blue silk threads and mix them with a dilute non-water soluble adhesive, suspend them in water, and then spray the water evenly onto your rag paper. Press the sheets between Teflon rollers and allow to dry.

3. Some parts of the bill are printed in sparkly, color-shifting ink. Your printer won't be able to reproduce this, the plastic security strip, or the watermark. However, you could copy counterfeiter Ricky Scott Nelson, who took real $1 and $5 bills, masked the serial numbers, Treasury and Federal Reserve Seals, and the words "This note is legal tender." Then he bleached the bills and printed $50 and $100 detailing over the tops.

4. Print the fronts of several test bills, altering the hue, color balance, saturation, and contrast until you get the best color and definition match. Repeat with the back of the bill.

5. Print a double-sided bill, and keep only those where the front and back are perfectly aligned.

6. Spend small quantities of your fake cash in locations with low chances of detection (e.g., at nightclubs, where the light is poor, and staff may be too busy to check). For larger quantities, use them in drug transactions, sell them to foreign black marketers or drug dealers to use in scams, convert them to large denomination chips in Las Vegas, or take them to currency exchanges in Mexico.

67. Create Crop Circles

According to some New Age groups, crop circles are messages from aliens or are extraterrestrial landing sites made by "tachyonic energy," a sort of weird cosmic vibe that creates and maintains order in the chaos of matter. However, the sane among us know that they are created by a group of (often inebriated) friends armed only with rope and some planks of wood.

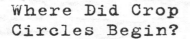

Where Did Crop Circles Begin?

Two British artists, Doug Bower and Dave Chorley started the craze. One summer evening in 1978 after a few pints at the bar, they made their first crop circle on their hands and knees with a four-foot metal bar. Their efforts were rewarded with worldwide interest, and they continued to make crop circles for over a decade.

How to Make an Alien Landing Strip

1. Choose your location carefully. The best place is a sloped field that can be seen from a road, so that a

maximum number of passers-by can be freaked out by its unique and mysterious beauty.

2. Use a PC and spend a long time planning your design and its execution, so that when you get in the field you won't be faced with an impossible task. A basic design should incorporate an arrangement of discs in a geometric formation. Gather a team of like-minded hoaxers from your local drinking establishment, and give everyone a designated area to work on.

3. Make your crop circle under cover of night during dry conditions, and access the field using an existing farm track. Your basic tool is a piece of wood with a hole drilled at each end, and a rope attached through the holes. Hold the rope loop while you flatten the corn forward and down, keeping one foot on the wooden bar.

4. To make a circle, one person stands in the center holding one end of the rope; a second person holds the other end of the rope to form the radius of the circle, and walks around the first person, flattening the corn to create the circumference. Then the wooden plank tool can be used to flatten the area inside the circle. You can also use a small lawn roller, available at most garden centers. To make more complex shapes, make construction lines by laying rope outlines.

5. When you've finished, add some extraterrestrial details such as melted iron filings which make convincing "meteorite particles," or scatter around some disemboweled cows. Complete your design just before dawn, then you can take a photo of it before all the "croppies" arrive. Make sure you remove all evidence of human involvement, including cigarette butts (assuming you are stupid enough to smoke around dry corn) and empty beer cans.

68. Make Moonshine

Moonshine, popskull, stumphole, ruckus juice, hillbilly pop, happy Sally: whatever you want to call it, making illegal alcohol is still one of the most enjoyable ways of breaking the law, evading federal taxes, and losing your eyesight. It takes lots of time and practice before you can whip up an impurity-free batch that won't do you serious damage. Use it in your lawnmower until you are confident enough to open a speakeasy.

Sprout the Corn

"Sprout" five pounds of shelled whole corn to convert the cornstarch into sugar. Put the corn into a container with a slow-drainage hole, cover with warm water, drape a cloth over the mouth, and leave it for three days (or until the sprouts are about two inches long), adding more warm water as required. Dry the sprouts and grind them to make cornmeal (alternatively, buy five pounds of cornmeal and skip this step).

Mash

Make a "mash" by adding twenty gallons of boiling water and twenty pounds of sugar to the cornmeal. When the mash has cooled to "warm" add one and a half ounces of yeast. Leave in a warm place for about three days to ferment (or until the mash stops bubbling). Now the mash has been converted to carbonic acid and alcohol and is called "sour mash."

Distillation

Distill the mash by heating it to 173°F in a copper moonshine still. At this temperature, the alcohol (ethanol) rises to the top of the still, and then travels along to the cooling part of the still, where it condenses again and can be collected. It will be a clear liquid the color of dark beer.

Singlings

The first liquid to condense from the still contains volatile oils, and should be discarded. After that, the liquid can be collected into glass jars called "singlings." The liquid collected at the end of the run is called "low wine" and is only about 10 percent proof, so it can be added to the mash barrel and distilled again. Stop distilling once a tablespoon of low wine thrown on a naked flame refuses to burn.

Distill Again, and Again

Empty the mash (it can be added to the next batch of grain). The ethanol collected in the first singlings will have the highest proof, and the proof level drops as the process continues. However, all the singlings will need to be distilled one or two more times to remove impurities. After three distillations, some of your singlings will contain ethanol up to 150 proof (that's about 75 percent alcohol).

69. Walk on Hot Coals

Common sense says that mind over matter just doesn't figure when it comes to flame grilling your feet. After all, when you toss a steak on the barbecue, it cooks regardless of whatever positive thoughts it is entertaining. Fire walking boils down to thermal conductivity and how you rake the coals; it has little to do with how you walk or what you're thinking, so this explanation is more of a "why it works" than a "how-to."

Leidenfrost Effect

This is named for Johann Gottlob Leidenfrost, who described the effect in his manuscript *A Tract About Some Qualities of Common Water* (1756). The Leidenfrost effect makes it possible for a person to plunge their wet hand briefly into a vat of molten lead without injury, to blow liquid nitrogen from their mouth, and many believe, to fire walk. Leidenfrost discovered that when a liquid comes into contact with a mass that is much hotter than the liquid's boiling point, instead of evaporating quickly, a thin layer of vapor forms between the liquid and the hot mass which acts as an insulator, increasing the time it takes to boil. Although there is disagreement about whether this applies to walking on hot coals, those who believe that the Leidenfrost effect comes into play here argue that sweat and normal body moisture on the soles of the feet turn to vapor and protect them from the high temperatures of the coals. Also, many fire walks take place on grass, so it is easy for the feet to pick up further moisture, especially if the grass is wet.

Poor Conduction

The most significant factor is the heat of the coals versus their ability to conduct that heat. Just because a material is red hot does not make it dangerous. For example, the heat shield tiles on the Space Shuttle are such poor conductors of thermal energy that you can handle them while they are glowing. Coals burn at approximately 600°C, but the surface heat will be absorbed by your feet, especially if the embers are wood, which is a poor conductor. If the coals were replaced with hot metal (an excellent conductor) you could kiss your feet goodbye. (Remember your piece of steak? That cooks on the barbecue because it is sitting on a griddle made of metal.) Also, the coals cool quickly when they are raked out over a wide area.

In short, so long as you keep up a steady pace, you can use the mantra "hot coals, hot coals, third degree burns" while you are walking, and you still won't get so much as a blister.

70. Sell Your Organs for Beer Money

Selling your organs can be a great way to make some extra money because one person's viscera is another person's vitality. Right now, about 90,000 men, women, and children in America need organ transplants and about sixteen people die every day because they don't get one, so it's practically your duty to offload some of your innards to subsidize your next kegger.

Is It Ethical?

Does the Pope shit in the woods? Of course it's ethical. What could be more ethical than a person of sound mind and body living in a liberal democracy and free market economy deciding they want beer more than one of their kidneys? A sick person wants a kidney more than money, so it's a mutually beneficial exchange, and after your fifth bottle of beer these ethical dilemmas become less important anyhow.

Is It Legal?

Are polar bears Catholic? No—the law forbids any money or other "valuable considerations" from changing hands in exchange for an organ donation. Also, more importantly, most organs may be donated only if a person is declared brain dead. That's precisely the reason why an illegal black market dealing organs is thriving, especially on college campuses, since dying rich people will pay huge sums to get their hands on tender young organs. Flip through the pages of any fashion magazine to see that the commodization of human bodies is already thriving, so what's the big deal?

Is It Painful?

Did flash-forwards ruin Season Four of *Lost*? Of course it's painful. Having a kidney removed is not only difficult and dangerous, it hurts a lot. Also, if your remaining kidney fails you, you're dead. And a month after the operation, you'll be in so much pain you'll wish the surgeon had removed both kidneys.

Have Kidney Will Travel

To have your organs harvested, you will likely have to go abroad where the rules are less strict. The number one destination is probably China because its government openly condones organ harvesting. Hospitals there headhunt foreigners and are prepared to pay up to $65,000 for a kidney. Also, check out Moldova, where the government has issued a ban but it is also directly involved with the trade. Other topnotch organ-trafficking destinations include India, Pakistan, Egypt, Israel, Russia, Singapore, Philippines, Colombia, Turkey, South Korea, and Taiwan.

71. Construct and Use a Beer Bong

Making and taking beer bongs is not only one of the most fun, efficient, and least labor-intensive ways of delivering beer to your stomach, it's also . . . nope, that's the only reason why it exists.

Materials

You can buy pre-assembled bongs cheaper than it costs to make your own, but that's like buying a generic PC from the store. When you've bought your own raw materials and customized your bong (funnel size/tube width), it becomes a much-loved member of the family. You should be able to get everything from the plumbing section of any hardware store. You'll need:

Funnel: translucent is best, so you can see the foam and clean it easily, and as large as possible (at least 2 beers worth). Try to find one with gradations on the side to show volume (if not, mark your own in ½ beer gradations with permanent marker).

Tubing: clear tubing, 2 to 2 ½ inches in diameter; this allows fast beer flow, but still fits comfortably

in the mouth. The tubing should be about 3 feet long for individual use or unlimited if you have helpers (e.g. someone to hold and fill the bong out the second floor window while you stand on the ground below).

Turn valve: fits snugly into the tube to control flow.

Prepare the Bong

Open the valve and rinse the bong with ice cold water—this reduces foam build-up. Close the valve and, holding the funnel and tubing at 45 degrees, slowly pour the beer down the side of the funnel to minimize foam, then hold the apparatus vertical and allow any foam to settle until it has risen to the top of the funnel, or above the required gradation, or better yet, until all the bubbles have gone.

Now Take It

Assume the position (get down on one knee) and hold the funnel above your head with the tube vertical. Expel air from your mouth (i.e. depress your cheeks) and then place the end of the tube in your mouth (or if your name is Steve-O, your rectum). Open the valve. Don't suck. The best way is to open your throat and let gravity do its work; if you can't, remember to keep swallowing, rather than just let your mouth fill up.

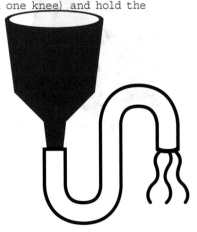

72. Grow Marijuana in Your Room

Growing marijuana indoors is harder than growing it outside. It requires at least eight hours of sunlight every day. However, it has the advantage of being concealed from nosey law enforcers like your RA and the cops, both of whom will take it off you and smoke it themselves. If you think about it for a moment, it won't surprise you to learn that marijuana is a weed. This means that it grows like . . . well, like a weed, as long as you provide the right conditions.

Plant Your Seeds

Soak your nice green seeds (if they are gray, they won't work) overnight in distilled water, and then plant them ½ inch deep with the pointy end up in an indoor starter box to germinate. The growing medium should be a mixture of fertilizer, soil, compost, and sand, so that it absorbs water well.

Transplant

When the sprouts are well established, transplant them into grow bags, allowing about one cubic foot of soil per plant and space the plants at least two feet apart. Make sure you leave plenty of soil around the roots, so you don't damage them. Water well before and after transplanting.

Ambient Conditions

The temperature around the plant should not exceed 75 degrees. Provide up to sixteen hours of "sunlight" (with a minimum of eight hours) each day using a 75 watt fluorescent strip light positioned about 1½ feet from the plants. Cover your dorm walls behind the plants with aluminum foil to reflect the light. Keep the room well ventilated.

Harvesting

Your crop will produce both male and female plants, both of which contain THC (the major psychoactive chemical compound, tetrahydrocannabinol). The male plants are generally tall with stout stems and a few leaves, and they have little buds which look like little nuts. The females just have white pubes. Harvest the male plants before they shed their pollen (unless you want the female to produce seeds). If the female plant is not pollinated, its flower will continue to grow and produce more THC than if it were allowed to produce seeds. Cut the plants at soil level.

Curing

Before you can smoke your weed, it must be dried. Place the leaves on a baking sheet and bake in the middle of a hot oven until they smoke and curl up. Remove them from the oven and store them somewhere cool until you are ready to get high.

73. Con Your Way Into the Space Program

If you dream of an exciting career that combines peeing in a bag with floating around a freezing vacuum, look no further than the space program. Aim for the stars! Not all astronauts are geniuses with IQs of 160; some are muscular jet pilots as well. However, some programs are easier to get into than others.

It Ain't Rocket Science

At NASA, which send shuttles up faster than Jim Carrey changes his facial expressions, you won't get past the receptionist, while over at the European Space Agency you can bribe all the security guards with a ripe Camembert and a packet of Gitanes (although it doesn't look like any of its rockets will make it into orbit until at least 2060). If you have a few hundred million to spare, you can always hitch a lift to the Space Station with the Russians.

G-force Unit

In most space programs, before they'll let you fly a rocket (or rather, grip the steering wheel and let the G-force wreck you while two million tons of volatile propellant explodes under your seat), you either have to be a super-fit pilot with a science degree who has clocked more than a thousand hours of experience in charge of a jet airplane, or spend several more years studying to be a payload specialist (all so you can fool around with a robotic arm, a skill any child can learn on a pick-and-grab machine in the mall). You will also be expected to be cool under pressure and scribble down lots of "gimble co-ordinates" like Gary Sinise in *Apollo 13*. Even then, if you get the sniffles, or are found to be too short (below 5' 4") or too tall (above 6' 3") you'll fail the height restriction and go back to flipping burgers. Clearly you need to know an extra trick to bump you to the front of the line.

SASPIS

Few people are aware that NASA is currently recruiting willing participants in a top-secret eugenics project called SASPIS which is jointly-funded by the CIA and the U.S. Census Bureau. All you have to do to qualify is pass an IQ test consisting of a short presentation: a Census agent projects onto the wall in letters two-feet high the words "Send All the Stupid People Into Space." When they turn on the lights and ask if you've changed your mind—here is the important part—make sure you say, "NO." Congratulations, you just won your ticket out of here, and can expect to be heading towards the

74. Talk Your Way Past a Border Guard

If you want to cross a border, the golden rule is don't cross the border guard. He stands between you and forward progress, so you have to play on his terms and stay calm, compliant and respectful, no matter what, even when you know you are being taken for a ride.

Borders can be very frustrating places, where you feel that things are out of your control, but remember that when the going gets tough you can at least control your own emotions and behavior. In many cases, your attitude dictates how you are treated. If you get impatient and start making demands, you can expect to be given the full five-star body and vehicle search, which is not a pleasant experience and can set you back hours.

Ten Ways to Keep Your Mind and Body Together

1. Be organized. Have all your passports, visas, and other travel documents ready for presentation. Being disorganized wastes the guards' time and they will waste yours in return, plus they will judge you for your sloppiness.

2. The same goes for your appearance—look smart (but not too smart—nothing says "hit me for a bribe" better than a $2,000 suit and Rolex). Men: have a shave—scruffy equals untrustworthy—and remove your sunglasses and hat.

3. Treat everyone with respect but don't be a pushover. If you suspect that you are being asked for a bribe, pretend you don't understand and ask for a receipt. Don't assume that the guards are low in the pecking order; in some countries they are important government officials.

4. Stick together. If one of you is asked to enter the post, make sure one of your party accompanies them, but don't leave your vehicle unattended.

5. Keep your trunk tidy; an untidy trunk can be all the excuse a guard needs to strip down your vehicle. If this happens, don't wander off for a smoke; remain with your wheels and keep vigilant for light-fingered guards.

6. Stay calm and focused. Hesitation or nerves will make you look like you have something to hide.

7. Find out the busiest crossing times (such as weekends and public vacations) and avoid them, otherwise you may incur overtime fees, or be kept waiting until they become payable.

8. Now is not the time to try out any of your wisecracks. Making a joke about how much dope you've got stashed in the tires is an invitation to have them cut open. Border crossing is a serious business. By all means laugh if the guard makes a joke, but save your one-liners for later.

9. If you own expensive equipment (wristwatch, camera, etc.) that looks new, carry a photocopy of the purchase receipt, otherwise it will be hard to prove that you aren't smuggling goods in or out of the country.

10. Don't stare. The guards may be carrying some neat looking automatic weapons, but if you eyeball them too much, they will get twitchy and suspicious.

75. Go Over Niagara Falls in a Barrel

And chance coming back in a box. Sixteen people have attempted the stunt and eleven have survived (two men have done it twice and lived). That's good odds, considering that Horseshoe Falls has a vertical drop of 170 feet (52 meters). No matter the materials you use for your "barrel" and how meticulous the planning, the stunt is still very dangerous so here's a quick checklist as you make your plans in the bar.

1. Avoid the American Falls, as there are too many rocks at the bottom. All successful attempts have been over the Horseshoe Falls (unfortunately this does require a trip over the border to Canada).

2. Despite the success rate, there have been some nasty injuries, such as those of Bobby Leach (the first person to use a steel barrel, way back in 1911). He broke his jaw and both kneecaps and spent six months in the hospital. Can you afford to be out of work for that long?

3. The main hazard is that the barrel will hit rocks and split open and then you'll either drown or get your body smashed by the water and the rocks. Most modern attempts have used materials such as rubber and metal, sometimes both. Experience shows that your barrel should be light

and strong. In 1984, Karel Soucek used lightweight wood and plastic, and some ballast in the bottom ensured he descended feet-first. However, if your container is too flimsy, like "The Thing" used by William "Red" Hill Jr. in 1951, it may survive the fall but break apart under the cascade of water. He died. In 1920, Charles Stevens (the third person to attempt it) strapped himself inside a very heavy oak barrel and tied an anvil to his feet for ballast. Don't do this. The anvil smashed through the bottom of the barrel taking him with it, leaving behind one of his arms. He also died.

4. Wood is good but rubber is better. In 1928, Jean Lussier used a six-foot rubber ball with thirty-two inner tubes reinforced with steel bands. He survived unharmed. Thirty-three years later, Nathan Boya used a steel sphere encased in six-ply rubber with similar results. Probably the best design was used in Steve Trotter's and Lori Martin's second successful attempt in 1995: two hot water tanks, surrounded by a thick layer of Kevlar; it was also the most expensive option, costing $19,000.

5. Take some sandwiches and air tanks, so you don't get hungry or suffocate waiting to be rescued. In 1930, George Stathakis suffocated after getting stuck behind the water curtain for 18 hours (his companion, a pet turtle, survived).

6. Even if you survive you will be fined up to a maximum of $10,000 plus court costs for "stunting without a license." (In 1995, Steve Trotter also spent 2 weeks in jail.)

Do it for the thrill but not for the fame. Before today, did you know the names of anyone who has gone before? Maybe the sixty-three-year-old retired school teacher Annie Edson Taylor who was the first person to attempt it (with her cat) in 1901, using a modified pickle barrel. But it didn't gain her the wealth and notoriety she so badly craved, and she died two decades later, broke. Plus her cat never forgave her.

76. Have Underground Cosmetic Surgery in Brazil

Plastic surgery tourism offers a vacation that pays for itself; you can recoup the cost by what you save in health care while enjoying an exotic vacation where you can pick up some unique souvenirs and leave your worries at Rio de Janeiro airport along with ten pounds of tummy fat on the return journey. Besides, it's got to be better booking two weeks abroad than to have to tell your boss you're having liposuction.

Where else can you enjoy sun, fun, and surgery at bargain basement prices (apart from Malaysia, Thailand, South Africa, Costa Rica, or the Philippines)? Brazil proudly receives clients from all over the world seeking the cheapest plastic surgeons this side of Kuala Lumpur. The country is famous for its stunning women and its international soccer players, so it is the natural place to experience body modification.

Quick Hands for Such a Big Fella

Most surgeons are licensed by the Brazilian Football Confederation (CBF) and they are currently ranked fifth by FIFA for buttock implants, liposculpture, and taking a dive in the penalty area. You can go under the knife confident in the knowledge that you are in the capable hands of doctors who serve five-time World Cup winners. All the doctors are mono-lingual, so that if you wake up paralysed on the operating table just blink your eyes rapidly to attract their attention and to let them know that you would like some more anaesthetic.

Take the Shot

As you would expect from a bustling South American capital, crime is a normal part of everyday life and no areas of the city or times of day are immune, but if you get shot here you'll be stitched up for a third of the price. However, make sure you remove all jewelry and other valuables from your person before the operation as an unconscious patient always attracts the attention of thieves.

What a Clinical Finish

The best time to visit is four days before Ash Wednesday; that way you can enjoy Carnival and then have surgery, leaving you plenty of R&R time before you fly home. Each procedure comes with a some-of-your-money-back guarantee that nearly all of the scars will be almost invisible to the naked eye at thirty paces.

77. Kill Your Computer

If your PC crashes at random intervals, you can germinate seeds while it boots up, or it is so old that you wish it would just die so you can move on with your life, here are some ways to hasten its demise. Don't be sentimental. Sure, you have enjoyed some epic multiplayer online gaming sessions together, and its hard drive has seen more hard-core pornography come and go than Hugh Hefner's closet. But some PCs are prime candidates for assisted suicide.

1. Power supplies account for about 30 percent of all dead-PC occurrences. Their job is to filter 240 volts down to bite-sized 12V, 5V, and 3.3V DC allocations that modern PCs need. So if you want to screw up your PC, buy a cheap power supply and don't use a surge protector (or just stick a chisel into it). With luck, you'll scorch some of the motherboard and toast the RAM. Alternatively, flick the little red self-destruct switch on the power supply: the one that changes between 115 and 230 volts.

2. Keep your PC on the floor and let it accumulate dust. Never vacuum on or near it. Eventually the cooling fan will get clogged up and your ICU will overheat. If you can't wait that long, just unplug the fan or remove the heatsink and the processor will cook itself to death in a matter of seconds.

3. Loosen some of the components, such as the RAM, so that it is seated incorrectly. When you boot up, it will short out and, ideally, melt the slot as well, filling the room with the smell of singed hair.

4. During a lightening storm, leave your PC plugged into the power supply, and the modem plugged into the wall. Hopefully, your house will get struck by lightning, frying not only your PC, but any other piece of electrical equipment that is plugged into the mains. Static electricity is also a PC killer. Rub your feet back and forth on a synthetic carpet while wearing shoes, then touch your mouse; you should get enough static electricity that shocks you and fries the mouse and keyboard. Open up the PC case and you can destroy computer components just by touching them, thanks to electrostatic discharge (ESD).

5. Overclocking is the act of increasing the speed of certain components in a computer beyond what is specified by the manufacturer. In some BIOS's you can alter your CPU speed and fry your computer without even taking the back off. When you boot your PC, enter your BIOS (usually by pressing Del, F1, or F10) then change your CPU speed or voltage to the highest number. Then sit back and wait for the sparks.

78. Become a Religious Icon

Long before you start building your fan base and drawing really big crowds, you need to ask yourself some tough questions. Being a Messiah isn't just about riding donkeys and performing miracles (though this will take up a lot of your time). It's a major lifestyle choice where every aspect of your personality will be brought into the public domain and placed under intense scrutiny. Plus, it's a highly competitive area, with new Messiahs ready to step into your sandals immediately after your inevitable crucifixion.

Your Image

Lose weight. Messiahs tend to be average to underweight. Accentuate with baggy clothing.

Wear comfortable shoes and grow a beard. Sadly, this rules out most women under the age of fifty, making the job of Messiah a very male-biased arena.

Put whitener on your teeth. Messiahs always have bright teeth.

Try to cut down on any bad habits like swearing, picking your nose, smoking, and having casual sex. You'll soon be dying for the sins of the world and you don't want to lessen the impact of your self-sacrifice by getting lung cancer or AIDS.

Create a Buzz

Relocate to a hot and dry country. For some reason Messiahs never really take off in places where average rainfall exceeds twenty inches per year.

The best way to build your status as Messiah is to deliberately shun publicity by avoiding large crowds. Take every opportunity to go fishing with a few close friends. Frequently lock yourself in the toilet and say you need time alone to think, or better still, wander off into the desert for a few weeks. (Make sure your agent knows where you are.) This introspective and enigmatic behavior will soon lead to a booking on the Late Show with David Letterman.

Call everyone "my child" but don't be patronizing. People hate that. Also, touch everyone you meet on the top of the head.

Start hanging out with prostitutes, the poor, the sick, and the unemployed. Not only will this make you appear compassionate, but after your death, it will be the money and blind hope of these unhappy, gullible, and disenfranchised folk that will quickly turn you into a global phenomenon.

Be Vague

If anyone asks you whether you are the Messiah, deny it (even if you really are). Then lock yourself in the toilet.

Tell everyone how great your dad's house is. They will assume you are talking about Heaven (don't mention that he lives in a motel in Detroit).

Use lots of metaphors when speaking to the crowds that inevitably form whenever you leave the house. Talk inaudibly. This will create an atmosphere of awed silence in your presence, while also making you appear humble. Popular topics of conversation include bread and sheep.

Perform Miracles

Do not attempt any "magic" tricks—everyone hates magicians. Stick to the basic repertoire of killing shrubs, healing the sick, and raising the dead.

Crucifixion

Just before your death it is good practice to throw a quiet dinner party for twelve of your closest friends. Make an effort—don't just offer them bread and wine—you'll look like a cheapskate. Also, don't freak them out by saying stuff like "Eat me" or they'll be reaching for their coats before you can say "transubstantiation."

Resurrection

Arrange for a friend to break into the mortuary after your death and steal your body.

79. Light a Fart on Fire

Do you really think there's more to lighting your farts than holding a naked flame next to your butt while you break wind? Well there isn't. A search for "fart light" on YouTube will return over 400 examples of guys with no prior training doing just that. However, here are three ways NOT to ignite an air biscuit:

Don't attempt to cut the cheese near a naked flame when you need to use the toilet, otherwise there's an increased risk of follow through. Here's an extreme example of what we mean:

www.metacafe.com/watch/313171/how_not_to_light_a_fart/

Do not use any artificial combustants such as deodorant aerosols:

www.metacafe.com/watch/305430/fire_in_the_hole_2/

Finally, don't attempt to ignite your flatus in company if you can't produce any gas. Because you're then you're going to look really dumb:

www.youtube.com/watch?v=F1PgIQU2yq8

After all, if you can't even manage to light a fart, what the hell can you do, dumb-ass?

80. Avoid Ridiculous State Laws

In Alabama, you can be arrested for operating a vehicle blindfolded, wearing a fake moustache that causes laughter in church, flicking boogers in the wind, or keeping an ice cream in your back pocket.

Alaskans are forbidden from pushing a live moose from an airplane, waking a bear to take a picture, or taking a kangaroo (even willingly) into a barber shop.

In Arizona, it is illegal to hunt camels, and a driver who removes or ignores barricades at a flooded wash faces a minimum $2,000 fine.

In Arkansas, it is illegal to mispronounce Arkansas.

In California, it is against the law for anyone to stop a child from jumping over puddles of water, and a city ordinance states anyone who detonates a nuclear device within city limits will be fined $500.

In Colorado, a woman can only wear a red dress on the streets before 7 P.M. Also, you can't drive a black car on Sunday in Denver.

You will break the law in Connecticut when your bicycle reaches speeds in excess of 65 mph or when you walk across the street on your hands.

In Delaware, "R" rated movies cannot be shown at drive-in theaters, and it is illegal to fly over any body of water without adequate provision of food and drink.

Florida women can be fined for falling asleep under a hair dryer, and in Miami it is illegal for anyone to imitate an animal. Sex with a porcupine (unless you are a porcupine) is also prohibited; in fact any form of sexual contact other than missionary position is a misdemeanor.

You can't tie a giraffe to a lamppost in Georgia, or keep your donkey in the bathtub. As if that wasn't bad enough, all sex toys are banned.

In Hawaii, you can be fined for not owning a boat or for sticking coins in your ears.

In Idaho, you can't ride a merry-go-round on a Sunday, or fish on a camel's back under any circumstances.

Illinois law expressly forbids giving lighted cigars to dogs, cats, and other domesticated pets. Eating in a restaurant that is on fire, peeing in your neighbor's mouth, and drinking beer out of a bucket while sitting on the curb are all off limits.

Indiana disallows bathing during the winter, or attending a cinema or theater or riding a public streetcar within four hours after eating garlic. All hotel sheets must be exactly ninety-nine inches long and eighty-one inches wide.

In Iowa, kisses may not last longer than five minutes, and a man with a moustache may not kiss a woman in public. Horses are forbidden to eat fire hydrants.

Kansas condemns the use of ice cream on cherry pie, whale hunting, snowball fights, and screaming at haunted houses.

A woman in Kentucky must get her husband's permission before buying a hat, and anyone who has been drinking is "sober" until he or she "cannot hold onto the ground."

In Louisiana, biting someone with your natural teeth is "simple assault," but if you have false teeth you will be charged with "aggravated assault." Having a pizza delivered to someone without their permission will land you with a $500 fine.

Maine prohibits leaving an airplane during a flight, leaving your Christmas decorations up too long, or walking down the street with your shoelaces untied.

You cannot swear while inside the city limits of Baltimore, Maryland; give or receive oral sex anywhere; or allow thistles to grow in your yard.

In Massachusetts, you are breaking the law if you get a tattoo or body piercing, eat more than three sandwiches at a wake, take a dump on your neighbor, or wear a goatee beard without paying for a license.

When in Michigan, you are prevented from using a decompression chamber to kill your dog, swearing in front of your wife and children, or letting your pig run free in Detroit unless it has a ring in its nose.

Minnesota law prohibits walking across the Minnesota-Wisconsin border with a duck on your head; giving or receiving oral sex; or having sex with your wife if your breath stinks of garlic, onions, or sardines.

In Mississippi, it is illegal to teach others the meaning of polygamy, to parent more than one illegitimate child, or to seduce a woman with a false promise of marriage.

The law in Missouri precludes the installation of bathtubs with four legs resembling animal paws in Kansas City, or the rescuing of women who are in their nightgowns by firemen in St. Louis.

81. Go BASE Jumping

The behavior that separates humans from other animals is that some of us seem to enjoy exposing ourselves to unnecessary risks. BASE jumping, which involves using a parachute to jump from fixed objects (rather than from an airplane) is one sport in which this peculiar trait can be expressed.

What Does BASE Stand For?

BASE was coined by a moviemaker Carl Boenish in 1978, neatly summing up the sort of locations from which you can expect to hurl yourself: it stands for Building, Antenna, Span (a bridge, arch, or dome), and Earth (a cliff or other natural formation). Critics of the "sport" point out that it can also stand for "Bones And Shit Everywhere." Unsurprisingly, BASE jumping's illustrious founder died on a cliff jump in 1984.

How Is It Different from Skydiving?

First, it's much more dangerous. It is recommended that you perform at least 150 skydives before attempting your first BASE jump. BASE jumps are usually made from much lower altitudes

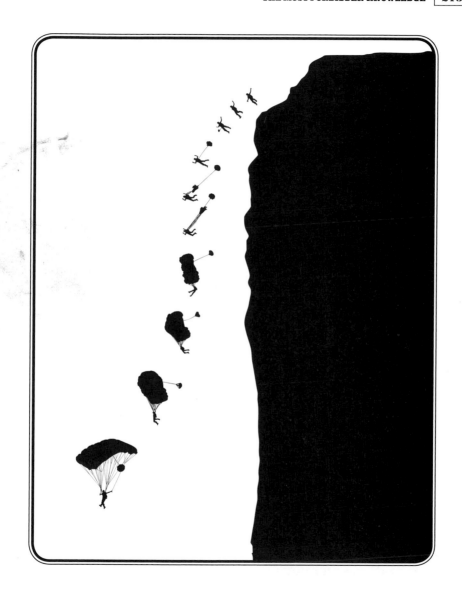

than skydives, although the current Guinness World Record for a BASE jump is from the 19,000-foot Trango cliff in Pakistan.

Skydivers use air flow to stabilize their position, so that they can open their parachute cleanly. BASE jumpers rarely reach terminal velocity, and therefore have less aerodynamic control, making chute deployment more hazardous. You'll also need a special parachute (and no backup—no time to use it), one that is bigger with a large pilot chute, and you'll only have a few seconds of freefall before chute deployment.

Where Can I Jump?

BASE jumping itself isn't illegal, but the trespassing you'll have to do to reach some of your jump platforms is. There is only one man-made structure in the U.S. where you can BASE jump legally year round: Perrine Bridge in Twin Falls, Idaho. Once a year, however, on the third Saturday in October, it's "Bridge Day" at the New River Gorge Bridge in Fayetteville, West Virginia, where over 800 jumps are made in a window of just six hours. Other than that, if you want to jump from the Willis Tower, it's up to you to get to the top without being arrested.

Apply for a Base Number

When you complete a jump you can apply for a "BASE number." The first (BASE-1) was awarded to Phil Smith of Houston, Texas, in 1981.

82. Become a Fake Medium

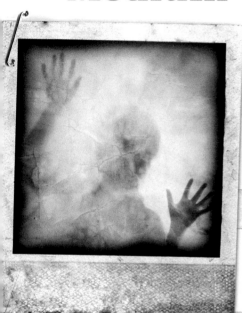

Here are some of the good old fashioned tricks that fake mediums used in their heyday. Incredibly these methods succeeded in fooling thousands of Victorians into parting with their cash in the belief that they were witnessing the manifestations of dead spirits.

Dim the Lights

Always perform your séance in a dark or nearly dark room. Tell your clients that this makes it easier for the spirits to manifest.

Spirit Cabinet

Hide all your magic tricks, props, and costumes in a large piece of furniture that has hidden compartments, or in a curtained-off area of the room. This is your "spirit cabinet." Explain that this will help you to attract, channel, and conserve spiritual forces. Allow your clients to view the cabinet, but make sure that the last person to inspect it is your assistant, who will plant the necessary equipment. Keep more wigs and makeup in a fake panel in your chair.

Ghosts

Get your assistant to materialize from a trapdoor in the floor or a sliding panel in the wall, or pretend to be a dead child by walking around the room on your knees.

Moving Objects

Floating spirits can be made by painting faces on inflated balloons. Attach objects by a fine thread to an adjustable fishing rod to make them move.

Spirit Music

Getting the spirit to play a musical instrument is an important part of the show. For example, make a violin play eerie notes by dangling a weight from a thread off the end of the table. The thread then passes over strings of the violin and then through the keyhole of a door, where it is pulled back and forth by your assistant in the next room.

Holding Hands

Holding hands around the table ensures that you cannot use them for trickery. However, if everyone alternates hand/wrist, then after the lights have gone down it is easy to make your neighbors believe they are each holding one of your hands, when in fact, they will be holding the hand and wrist of the same arm, leaving the other free for wielding your fishing rod, etc.

Ectoplasm

Spirit forms are made of "ectoplasm," which is a weird wispy substance that often emanates from a top-notch medium. Make fake ectoplasm from egg white, mixtures of soap, chewed paper, silk, or cheesecloth. Secrete it inside your mouth, and pull it out and wave it around at an opportune moment.

83. Break Bricks with Your Hands

Breaking bricks with your hands requires impeccable technique and considerable mental focus. The three basic principles are having self belief, hitting the brick as fast as possible, and minimizing the contact surface of the blow to maximize force.

Stance

With the soles of your feet firmly on the ground, bend your knees to lower your center of gravity. This is the solid base from which you can generate the power and speed to break bricks.

Intense Focus

Place both of your hands on the surface of the brick, and focus intently on the point through which you intend to strike. Aim for a target underneath the center of the brick. Maintain this eye contact until your hand has smashed through the masonry.

Speed and Fluidity

Move fast and with natural ease. Raise your striking hand backwards behind your head in a natural arc, while keeping your other hand on the brick. This is your backswing: it focuses your energy and keeps you fluid.

Turn your hips away from the target, and then bring them back again to transfer this torque energy into a striking force. Slice downward with a karate-chop hand as fast as you can in a natural arc, and tighten the muscles of the hand as it slices through the surface of the brick.

As your striking hand comes down, drive the other hand backwards in a circular movement to balance your body and to increase your power.

Contact Surface

The part of your hand that makes contact is the small bone just below your little finger (the fifth metacarpal). Human bone can withstand forty times more stress than concrete, while the muscle, tendons, ligaments, and soft tissue in the hand disperse the energy of the impact up through the arm so that you do not injure yourself.

The more momentum your hand has, the more force it can generate, and when that force is delivered through a small point of contact, it is concentrated with devastating results.

84. Exercise Your Squatter's Rights

In the U.S., squatting laws vary from state to state, but usually your presence won't be tolerated for very long. The legal property owner and/or neighbors will inform the authorities, and then the police will bust your ass for trespassing and kick you off the property. However, there are a few things you can do to tip the scales in your favor.

Entering the Property

There are two types of squat: "back window" and "front door." In the first, you come and go without being seen so no one knows you are there. In the second, you don't make any effort to hide your comings and goings.

When entering the property for the first time, do not leave any signs of forced entry. Breaking into a house is a criminal offense (such as forcing locks, breaking windows, etc). However, unscrewing a padlock bracket and then hiding it is not. The burden of proof will be on the owner to prove that there was a lock there. It is unlikely that he will have taken photographs of it.

Hide the Trespassing Signs

Remove and hide any signs which warn against trespassing. Again, the burden of proof is on the owner to show that all reasonable efforts were made to alert trespassers that they are unwelcome, and if you plead the Fifth, even though everyone knows that the signs were there, they can't prove that you saw or removed them. However, you will still be considered a trespasser against the owner. In legal terms, what you are doing is called "adverse possession" which is a form of civil trespass unless you fulfill certain legal requirements.

Stay for a Looong Time

To keep a property you must continuously possess it for several years (this varies from state to state) against the owner's will and pay all the property taxes.

As a squatter, you have no rights as a tenant, but you do have a Constitutional right to "due process of law," which means that the owner will have to take you to trial before you can be evicted, so long as the police don't rule that you are in the process of breaking and entering and remove you. Don't cause any criminal damage because you may be forced to pay damages to the owner.

85. Sneak Into Mecca

Mecca is in Saudi Arabia and is Islam's holiest city. It is the birthplace of the prophet Muhammad, the founder of the Islamic faith, and the place towards which Muslims around the globe face five times daily when they pray. Only Muslims are allowed into Mecca (as well as Islam's other holy city, Medina, the burial place of Muhammad, 210 miles northwest). Any non-Muslims caught in either city face dire consequences, either execution by the Saudi authorities, or even spontaneous death at the hands of an angry mob.

Book Burning

You may think this is unfair and retrograde, since the holy cities of Jerusalem and Rome are open to all, regardless of their religion, and you'd be right, but you have been warned and we in no way encourage you to do this. If you do, leave this book at home. Seriously. In fact, burn it: the last thing anyone needs right now is another Fatwah. Also, it's best to avoid the week of Hajj (the 8th to 12th day of *Dhu al-Hijjah*, the 12th month of the Islamic calendar), unless you want to become one of the hundreds of devout pilgrims who are trampled to death each year in the religious mayhem.

Infidel Explorers

A handful of infidel explorers have traveled in secret to Mecca and lived to tell the tale; the most famous was Sir Richard Burton who published *Personal Narrative of a Pilgrimage to al-Madinah & Meccah* in 1855 and claimed to be the "only living European who has found his way to the Head Quarters of the Muslim Faith." He went deep undercover, living as a dervish (a Sufi mendicant ascetic) in Sind and studied every aspect of Muslim culture, even apprenticing himself to a blacksmith to learn how to make horseshoes.

Grow a Beard

You don't have to go to these extremes. If you come from a country like the U.S. where religion does not appear on your passport, then in theory you should just need to grow a beard, wear a cream-colored *abaya* (or *hijab* if you are female), and gain some knowledge of Islam so you know which way to walk (counter-clockwise) around a large black cube called the Ka'bah, Islam's most sacred monument, and when to lower your head to the ground in prayer.

Mosque-See

When you arrive in Mecca, unload your luggage at the hotel and go straight to the Grand Mosque (Masjid al-Haram). Make sure you enter with the right foot first and keep your gaze lowered until you have a clear view of the Ka'bah. Then place your hands together and start praying. When you get home tell nobody what you've done, and definitely don't write a book about it.

86. Fly for Free

Imagine if you could fly anywhere in the world free of charge, with no boarding lines and no hassle. Well, imagine you're a world leader or an airline pilot then because for most of us there's no such thing as a free lunch. Or is there?

Get Born on a Plane

Being born on a plane used to guarantee free air travel for life; it's less likely these days because no airline allows passengers to fly if they are more than thirty-two weeks pregnant without a doctor's note, and not at all beyond thirty-six weeks. In any case, that was largely an urban myth, since there have only been two recorded incidents of a baby being awarded free flights for life. This is the exception, not the rule. Anyway, that's no good for you because you've already been born.

Get Bumped

Every day hundreds of people get free plane tickets from major airlines. These people agree to be bumped onto a later flight when too many passenger turn up for the scheduled flight (all flights are generally overbooked by 10 percent, to allow for no-shows). If the airline can't find you another flight leaving within the hour, then you will get at least $500 off your next flight, plus a coupon for about $100. Just before boarding, the airline will make an announcement asking if anyone agrees to step off. Make sure you have flexible travel arrangements so you can take advantage of the offer. Increase your chances further by volunteering to get bumped when you first check in.

Collect Air Miles on Your Credit Card

Lots of credit cards offer air miles for every dollar that you spend on the card. If you spend a gazillion dollars on your credit card you'll get a free ticket. However, be warned that some of these cards have very high interest rates (as high as 50 percent), so make sure you set up a direct debit to pay off the balance every month without fail to avoid any interest. Many stores also do loyalty cards that offer air miles.

Date a Pilot or Flight Attendant

Airline crews have a quota of free tickets for themselves and their family. Don't get married though, because you'll spend evenings alone, eating pizza in front of endless reruns of *CSI*, while your partner flies around the world. Pay attention—that's the exact opposite of what we're trying to achieve here!

Pretend to Have Cancer

That's more like it. There are several organizations that pay for flights for people to travel to their cancer treatment such as the Air Charity Network, or the Corporate Angel Network, to name but two. Shave your hair off and jump on the gravy plane. If you want to keep your hair, Lifeline Pilots caters to other illnesses too.

Become an Air Courier

Becoming an air courier is very easy. You just have to dress well and collect a parcel from the airline, and deliver it safely to your destination. Join the International Association of Air Travel Couriers (IAATC) and have a clean passport. Most carriers allow only one courier per flight, so two of you wouldn't be able to travel this way for free.

Mail Yourself

Get a friend to duct tape you into a sturdy box, and ship you to your destination by air freight. Take plenty of bottled water (drink the water and pee in the empty bottles) and wrap up warm because temperatures in the hold will reach well below zero.

87. Smuggle Illegal Immigrants in Your Truck

If you are a truck driver, there's no secret to smuggling human cargo. In fact, it's easier not to, as truckers frequently face crippling fines for each immigrant that falls out of their rig when they have crossed a border. Although, many of them claim ignorance. If you can't beat them, join them, and you can use the same defense if you get caught.

If You Can't Beat 'Em

You can make good money smuggling people from Mexico to the U.S. (up to $10,000 each) and in Europe (at least a year's salary). Patras in Greece is one of the prime routes used by smuggling gangs from Greece to Italy, with people from as far away as Afghanistan and Iraq looking for a ride. However, recently the checking regime has stepped it up. Still, the chances are if you are doing that route anyway, you will end up with some unwanted guests, so why not make some money for the risks you are taking? This also increases the chance of you reaching your destination without having the ropes and elastic holdings slashed to pieces as the stowaways gain entry. If you get caught, your stowaways should claim political asylum; that will take some of the heat off you.

Channel Crossing

If you are smuggling for the money rather than humanitarian purposes, you can make a fast buck on the route from France into the UK. The French will wave you through because they can't face the paperwork involved in catching illegals on their side of the Channel, especially during lunchtime. UK customs officials use sniffer dogs as well as carbon-dioxide and heartbeat detectors to catch stowaways. However, if there is something important on TV they won't search you, so try to time your journey to coincide with a soccer cup final, a royal wedding/funeral, or any Friday evening during the summer months (*Big Brother* eviction night).

Coming Up for Air

Keep the air vents open during the transporting, and fill up with gas in case you get into a police chase. Once you arrive at your destination, hand back passports to your passengers (you remembered to confiscate them earlier, right?). Don't smuggle more than twenty-five people at a time because otherwise they could run out of air or get carbon-monoxide poisoning, and even if they all survive you'll never get rid of the smell.

88. Land an Airplane in Open Water

If you want to play the Land-an-Airbus-320-on-the-Hudson game, or any body of water for that matter, it's not as easy as it looks. Once you've lost both engines, the only chance you've got of walking away alive is to get the nose down and glide so that when you hit the water the wings are producing very little lift while your forward motion is as slow as possible in order to pull off a low-speed, low-impact landing.

Gliding by the Seat of Your Pants

It might not surprise you to learn that airliners are not designed for gliding. A typical glider has a glide ratio of 30 or 60 to 1 which means that for every mile of altitude it can travel for 30 or 60 miles before it lands. An Airbus 320 has a fraction of that. If you lose power at 5,000 feet, you'll have about four or five minutes to land, so you've got to think really fast.

Here's what to do:

1. Send a mayday call to air traffic control and inform them that you intend to land in the water.

2. Tell the cabin crew and passengers to prepare for a crash landing.

3. Keep the landing gear stowed to make the bottom of the plane more like the hull of a boat. This will aid a smooth landing, and stops warning sirens from going off as the plane gets closer to the ground.

4. Turn off the air-conditioning to equalize the cabin pressure to match that on the outside.

5. Your most pressing concern is to slow the aircraft down. Extend the wing flaps fully and as you approach the water your speed is crucial—too fast and you will break up on impact; too slow and the plane will "stall," the wings will lose their lift, and the plane will simply drop out of the air and break apart.

6. As you bring the plane into land, lift the nose up to twelve degrees, which is higher than a normal runway landing, and lower the tail end. You must land the plane absolutely level, otherwise the plane can break apart on impact, or one wing will clip the water sending the plane into a cartwheel. Try to skim the surface of the water like a pebble.

7. Once you have landed, close all air vents and openings to keep the aircraft buoyant in the water. The plane is designed to float long enough to evacuate your passengers.

8. Look on the bright side—things could have been a lot worse: you could have landed at LAX.

89. Eat Blowfish in Japan

As culinary games of Russian roulette go, you can't live more dangerously than eating fugu—Japanese blowfish—a delicacy so poisonous that when prepared wrongly, the smallest amount of its venom can kill an adult human in less than thirty minutes (the ovaries, muscles, and liver contain a deadly poison). Here are a few tips to reduce the risk that you'll end the evening in respiratory and cardiac failure. However, your heart will miss a few beats when you see the bill: at the best restaurants one one serving of fugu can cost up to $250 per person.

Sleeping with the Fishes

In Japan, about 10,000 tons of blowfish are consumed each year, but fatalities are actually on the decline as the strict laws and licences which govern preparation of the dish have been tightened.

Call up the restaurant in advance and warn them that you will be ordering fugu. Preparation is such an art that the restaurant may have to bring in a specialized sushi chef, so give them plenty of notice. Unless you are a valued and regular customer, any restaurant that is prepared to serve you fugu without a reservation should be avoided.

Fugu sashimi is very filling, and although it is very expensive, the portion size is usually enough to satisfy two diners. Eat at the sushi bar rather than the table so that you can see it being prepared; these moments may be your last on earth, so savor them.

Delicate Taste

The fugu will be served in small thin strips with a radish dip accompaniment and a lime wedge. Only squirt on a few drops of lime (*sudachi*), and don't ruin the delicate taste with heaps of soy sauce (not only will you destroy the flavor, you'll appear uncouth). Eat slowly and wait for your lips and tongue to start tingling. This is normal, and not a sign that you are about to die; although if you lose feeling in your mouth or tongue, it's time to call an ambulance. You'll be dead by the time it arrives, but why not.

Other Fish to Fry

There are about a hundred kinds of fugu worldwide, but the most poisonous, expensive, and delicious variety is *Tora-fugu*, and the best season to eat it is during the winter (when you will pay a premium).

n°: 23458403
26 NOV. 1998
Jamaïca

90. Kill a Vampire

You've watched endless episodes of *Buffy the Vampire Slayer*, you've studied Bram Stoker's *Dracula* (including the novel, the play, the musical, the film, and even the novelization of Francis Ford Coppola's movie. You've played BloodRayne a dozen times, and the idea of a *World of Darkness* MMORPG (Massively Multiplayer Online Role-Playing Games) makes you drool. You even named the twins Jonathan and Mina.

But you don't know jack about vampires. No one does. Sure, we have dozens of legends about vampires and thousands of stories, but that's just the trouble. Not all of them can be right. And being wrong when you're facing down a thousand-year-old excuse for a human tick can be the kiss (and bite) of death.

Protective Measures

Vampires are fast, mean, and nasty, and they have the advantage of supernatural powers and potentially centuries of experience on their side. You have a handful of dusty legends (the ones you can remember) and the fact you probably won't really believe you've encountered a vampire until the moment before you're dead. (In case you're still stunned, neither of those works in your favor.)

Since you don't know for sure what you're up against, stock up on all the standards and double or triple up on them. Start with garlic, holy water, crosses, and anything else your favorite myths mention. Gather wooden stakes by the cord.

Add traditional weapons to your armory too: guns, knives, grenades, and more. Vampires are famous for making the living do their bidding, and that Super Soaker filled with holy water is only going to make such minions mad and wet.

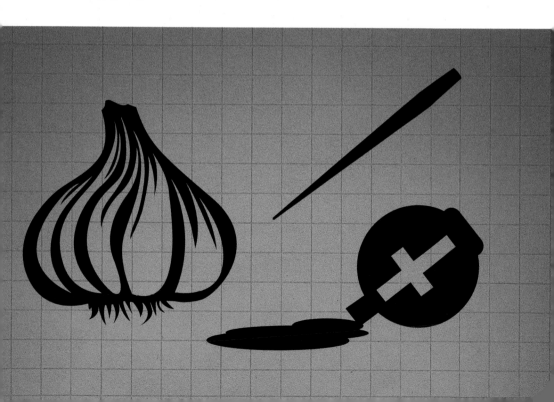

Elimination Strategies

When you finally face down a bloodsucker, start with the simplest methods and then pile on the pain until you find something that works. Once you figure that out, hammer at it over and over until every vampire in your zip code is a pile of ash. Most myths agree that a stake through the heart makes for a fine start for vampire extermination. In some stories, that's enough to put another notch on your cross. In Dracula though, a stake only pins the vampire down like a pin through a butterfly. To kill the beast, you then need to cut off its head, stuff its mouth with garlic, and cremate the remains. If you have the time, go with the most elaborate methods. As an undead creature, the vampire has already cheated death once. You need to make sure it doesn't get that chance again. But if you're hard pressed, just stake every vampire down and then go back and finish them off properly as soon as you can.

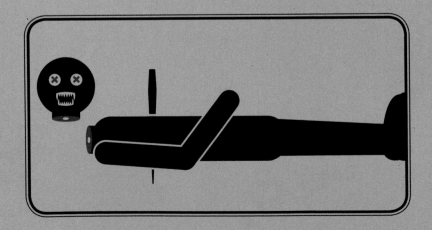

91. Beat a Breathalyzer

You've just been pulled over on your way back home after attending Midnight Mass at St. Jude's, and you're afraid that you might have sampled a bit too much of the sacramental wine before you got behind the wheel. Father Fred might absolve your sin after a proper confession and act of contrition, but the local law isn't likely to be so forgiving.

Don't Drink or Don't Drive

You don't need Oprah or MADD to tell you you're an idiot if you drink and drive, so we won't hammer that home here. Let's just say the best, most foolproof way to beat a breathalyzer is to never have to take one. If you must drive, don't drink. If you must drink, don't drive.

Can You Refuse?

Sure. The cops can't throw you to the ground and shove a breathalyzer in your mouth, then punch you in the gut until you expel your gin-soaked breath into the gadget. Well, they could, but they don't have to.

Every state has an implied consent law that says that if you have a driver's license you must consent to a breathalyzer test after being pulled over. Refusing to take one can be used against you in a court of law and often carries harsh criminal penalties of its own.

It's usually better to go along with the request and hope you're not as drunk as you fear.

What Might Work

Breathalyzers test the amount of alcohol in the air in your lungs. If you can get rid of some of that air, you might be able to reduce the amount that the breathalyzer can pick up by as much as 10%. To do this, try hyperventilating. Just don't pass out at the wheel as you do it. That won't help your case.

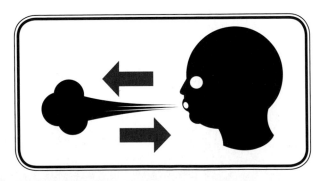

What Won't Work

Just about anything else. The most common attempts involve putting something in your mouth to try to fool the breathalyzer. People have tried pennies, mints, onions, breath spray, mouthwash, batteries, cardboard, underwear, and even their own shit.

Since the breathalyzer tests the air in your lungs instead of your mouth, none of these methods have any chance of working. In fact, some breath sprays and mouthwashes actually contain alcohol and can cause readings to look even worse.

92. Restart a Stopped Heart

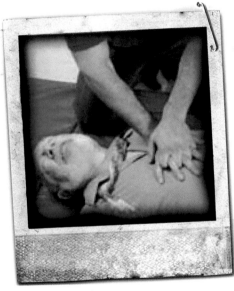

If you suddenly find yourself in a scene straight out of *Pulp Fiction* and your mob boss's girlfriend collapses to the ground with a stopped heart, what can you do? Especially if you don't happen to have a savvy drug dealer pal to hand you a needle filled with adrenaline and talk you through it?

Believe it or not, you have a number of options.

Call 9-1-1

If you don't have any clue about what to do, call 9-1-1 first. Turn on the speakerphone function on your phone, if you have one. You'll need your hands free if you want to follow the instructions of the emergency operator.

People tend to forget things in moments of stress, and this will be no exception. In a pinch, the operator might be able to help you with questions like, "How many compressions in a row in CPR?" Assuming you don't have this book with you at the time, of course.

Try CPR

The first thing most sane people would attempt in such a situation is to perform CPR. If you slept through your first-aid class (or never bothered to take one), that stands for Cardio-Pulmonary Resuscitation. "Cardio" means "heart," "Pulmonary" means "lungs," and "Resuscitation" means "getting them going again."

CPR is a series of chest compressions and breaths. Performed correctly, they can keep your friend alive until the ambulance arrives and the EMTs can take over. If you're lucky, it might even restart a stopped heart.

CPR is performed in a series of steps:

1. Pump the chest thirty times by placing the heel of your hand in the center of the person's chest, putting your other hand on top of that one, and pressing the chest down two inches at a rate of 100 per minute.

2. Tilt the person's head back and lift his chin to open the airway.

3. Pinch his nose closed, take a normal breath, cover the person's mouth with yours and blow out your breath until you see his chest rise. Go ahead and give another breath, taking about one second per breath.

4. Repeat steps 1 through 3 until help arrives.

Look for a Defibrillator

Lots of public places now feature AEDs (Automated External Defibrillators). If you don't see one when you need it, ask. Stress causes people to forget they're standing next to such things.

Follow the instructions on the AED to the letter. These are designed to be easy and safe to use. Once you attach the pads to the patient, the machine analyzes the attached heartbeat and delivers a shock designed to restart it.

Don't mess around with a defibrillator just for fun. The same shock that can start a stopped heart can just as easily stop a beating heart.

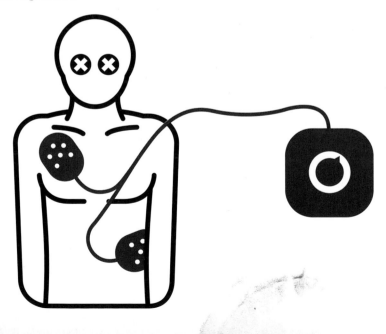

93. Challenge Someone to a Duel

When someone insults you, either reach for your weapon and teach them some manners, or elect to settle the dispute like a gentleman, with a test of courage, nerve, character, and personal honor: pistols at dawn.

Demand Satisfaction

Challenge someone to a duel by demanding "satisfaction" from them accompanied by an insulting gesture. In past times, this was usually slapping them in the face with a glove, however, mooning or giving them the bird is also acceptable. If they decline the challenge, they must issue a personal and, in some cases, a public apology.

Appoint a Second

Appoint a trusted friend to be your "second." His first job will be to liaise with your opponent's second to see if the dispute can be settled amicably without the need for a duel. Before the duel, your second is responsible for loading your pistol and ensuring that your opponent isn't cheating (e.g., by wearing concealed body armor or using an assault rifle). If you are unable to take part in the duel, your second should stand in for you.

Pistols at Dawn

You and your opponent begin back to back, at dawn (usually on a grassy knoll, next to a gnarled old tree surrounded by swirling mist). Since a duel is a private affair between the two individuals concerned, only they, their seconds, and a referee should be present. One of the seconds (or referee if you have one) calls the order "March," the duelists walk an agreed number of paces, then turn and fire.

If you fire and miss, you must allow the other person to take their shot. If they choose to fire in the air, rather than at you, they win the right to refuse future challenges.

The duel can either be to the death or can be called after first blood has been drawn. In other words, the first person to bleed loses.

94. Survive in a Foreign Jail

You disembark from the airplane after a grueling long-haul flight. All you want to do is get to your hotel, take a bath, and sleep for twelve hours. No such luck. There's a welcoming party of grim-faced drug officers waiting to drag you off to jail. You should have packed your own bags, you moron. Now what do you do?

Here's how to survive your own nightmare version of *Midnight Express*.

They Hang Drug Smugglers, Don't They?

Some do (Turkey, Thailand, Malaysia, Singapore, Indonesia, Iran, and Algeria), but many countries have mandatory prison sentences ranging from seven years to life, without the possibility of parole for drug violations. Unfortunately, there is very little that anyone can do to help you if you are caught with drugs. If you've told someone at home when to expect you back, you have a chance that they will report you "missing" to your embassy. You can't rely on "one phone call" in a foreign lockup situation. So you'd better shut up and do your time.

Contact the U.S. Embassy

If you are arrested and are carrying a U.S. passport, you have the right to contact the American embassy immediately. When an American has been arrested or detained, the local police are obliged to contact the nearest U.S. embassy.

What Can an Embassy Official Do for You?

So long as they know where you are, they can visit you in jail; they can give you a list of local lawyers (but they can't assume responsibility for their integrity—in other words, they could be crooked or incompetent); they can notify your family and friends; and they can intercede with local authorities to insure that your rights are being observed (under local law, that is—these may well be very different from what you would expect at home).

What Can't an Embassy Do?

It can't demand that you be released and expatriated, nor can it represent you at trial, give legal advice, or pay any fines or legal fees.

Cash and Cigarettes

On the inside, cash and cigarettes are essential commodities; they can get you anything from better food (instead of starvation rations) to protection and even sex. Using these as bribes may even get you released.

Learn the Language and Get to Know People

If you get thrown in for a long time, learn the language, culture, and customs of the people, and use that knowledge.

Keep Your Head Down

You may be a mule, but don't be a donkey as well. The last thing you need is for the goon squad to single you out as a troublemaker. If you want to have the crap beaten out of you or spend weeks naked in solitary confinement with nothing but a filthy mattress, go ahead and act like a big shot. If you're sensible, stick to the rules and don't do anything to get noticed.

95. Become a Computer Hacker

So you've decided to become a computer hacker but you don't know where to start. The most important quality a hacker needs is curiosity, because this fuels the development of your skills. If you're a person who instinctively wants to know how things work, likes stripping stuff down and building it up again, and loves problem-solving, then you have the beginnings of the hacker mindset.

You don't become a hacker overnight. It takes years of dedication and of soaking up information from every possible source: books, the Internet, newsgroups, etc. Back in 1996, a hacker named Eric Steven Raymond wrote a web document about hacking that many hackers consider definitive: see *www.catb.org/~esr/faqs/hacker-howto .html* for an updated version.

1. **Learn how to program. Start with Perl in Unix, or Visual Basic and Java in Windows, though hacking in Windows is very limiting. Then learn C, the core language of Unix, and move on to C++, which is closely related to it. The more programming languages you learn, the more options you'll have because you can compare how they work, and**

each language is suited to different tasks. The best way to learn a computer language is to immerse yourself in the environment and use it, contact others who are using it, share code and ideas, and live and breathe open source software.

2. Learn how to run an open source operating system like Unix/Linux. Install Linux or one of the BSD-Unixes and install it on a personal machine. Then you can play around without destroying your other work. Unix is the operating system of the Internet, so you have to know it to be able to hack.

3. Learn about data communication, networks, and how computers talk to each other. The best way to learn about the World Wide Web is to learn HTML and write lots of web pages.

4. Get out there in the hacker community; go on newsgroups and talk to people, join user groups and contribute to the group (rather than just asking "How do I hack?"). Share what you learn and others will share with you. No hacker is an island. To be part of the hacking community you have to identify with its goals and values, which you can only learn and attach importance to by becoming involved.

5. Set yourself projects and follow through with them. If you write a bit of code that solves a specific problem, share it with others.

6. Never stop broadening your knowledge and allowing your curiosity to guide your learning.

7. If you're a true hacker, you won't need any of this advice, because you'll already be doing it.

96. Make a Perfect Getaway

If you've just robbed a bank and need to make a fast getaway, here are some useful techniques to evade capture by the authorities.

Choose the Right Car

You can use evasive driving techniques with most cars, but not jeeps or pickup trucks, as they can roll easily during heavy cornering. The best getaway cars are powerful, easy to handle, and reliable, like a BMW M5 or a Mercedes, with an automatic transmission and bullet-resistant, run-flat tires. Avoid high-performance cars like Ferraris and Lamborghinis—it is easy to lose control of these.

Losing a Tail

If you are being chased by cops, shake them off your tail by cutting across four lanes of traffic on the highway and take the exit (this won't deter a helicopter); or after turning a blind corner, turn 180 degrees using a handbrake turn, then take off in the opposite direction.

Taking Corners

When approaching a corner, taking a late apex enables you to exit the corner at greater speed than if you had taken an earlier apex. However, if you are being followed you run the risk of being overtaken on the inside.

Knock Another Car off the Road

If you are behind your victim, ram their bumper on the left side with the right side of your car. You should be traveling about 20 mph faster than the car in front. This will make the other car veer to the right and go into a skid.

Alternatively, you can run him off the road by pulling alongside his car to the right so that the center of your car is in line with his front tires, then steer left and press your car against his to steer him off the road. Needless to say, you should never let anyone pull up alongside you, as they will be able to perform these same maneuvers on you.

Roadblocks

If you cannot escape a stationary roadblock by turning around, then you may have to ram it. To ram a two-car roadblock:

1. Slow down, almost to a halt. This makes the cops think you are about to give yourself up.

2. Hit the gas suddenly and ram right in the middle of the two cars, maintaining your speed during the collision. Your impact speed should be between 15 and 30 mph.

3. After passing the roadblock, accelerate as quickly as possible and drive away.

97. Go AWOL from the Armed Forces

Armed service personnel are classed as going Absent Without Official Leave or AWOL when they are absent from their post without a valid pass or leave. The U.S. Marine Corps and Navy call it Unauthorized Absence, or "UA."

What Happens Next?

When you have been AWOL for thirty days, you will be dropped from your unit rolls and listed as a deserter. Under U.S. military law, desertion is not determined by the length of time a person has spent from the unit, but rather if there is a clear intent not to return or if there is intent to avoid dangerous duty or evade important responsibility. It's a clear indication you do not intend to return to your unit if you leave and then sign on with the same branch of service while keeping your previous unit a secret, or if you join a foreign armed force not authorized by the U.S.

Top Security Clearance

If you go AWOL and you have top security clearance, you will automatically be classified as a deserter because of the sensitive nature of the information you had access to.

Missing Movement

This is similar to going AWOL but is much more serious and is a violation of the 87th article of the Uniform Code of Military Justice. It occurs when you fail to arrive at a fixed time to deploy with your unit, ship, or aircraft.

Your Punishment

Before the Civil War, army deserters were flogged, and in the late nineteenth century they were tattooed and branded. The maximum U.S. penalty for desertion in wartime is death.

Persons considered AWOL/UA may be punished with non-judicial punishment (NJP; called "office hours" in the Marines). They are usually punished by court-martial for repeat or more severe offenses. However, if your father is a U.S. congressman from Texas and future President of the United States, then your superiors will never discipline you even if you blow off your military duties for seventeen months.

98. Sleep with Your Professors

It's worth considering that professors are older versions of nerds you wouldn't have dreamed of dating in high school. But the power dynamic and the pay check give them an edge, plus the thrill of doing something forbidden. Don't expect to discover anything deeper than a brief spell of mutual gratification.

Wait Until the Grades Are In

It is generally a bad idea to hit on your professors while you are still taking their courses. Most colleges consider this grossly unprofessional and a sackable offense, so the stakes will usually be too high—unless you are really hot and leave them with no doubt about your intentions and your discretion. The best time to hook up is after you get your grade, then no one can say that you traded sex for that A. However, that shouldn't stop you from flirting during the whole semester. Sit up front; wear a short skirt if you're a woman; maintain eye contact during lectures; touch their arm or leg during conversation. You could even lick your lips, or have a wardrobe malfunction (it's hard to misinterpret a nip slip, or a ball sack exposure).

Sexual Harassment

During the '60s, professors and students were all jumping in and out of each other's beds, but in the modern climate of sexual harassment, professors have to be very careful about how they behave. That means that you've got to make your interest very clear. If you are a woman, you will have to make all the moves, rather than drop a few hints and wait for him to move in on you.

Behind Closed Doors

At the end of the course, after the grades are in, make an appointment to see your professor. Tell them how much you enjoyed their course, that you trust and respect their opinion, so you would like help with a personal matter. Ask if you can close their door; if they refuse, then they aren't interested. Say you have a friend who wants to become involved with their professor and doesn't know what to do. If your professor says it's a bad idea, you know where you stand. If they are undecided, then they still need convincing that you are interested and that you won't tell everyone. If they have positive response, suggest a bar somewhere quiet where you can continue your discussion and take it from there.

99. Get Into Secret Societies

If you're the sort of person who can't enjoy a party for fear of missing out on a better one somewhere else, where the dress code is BMBG ("black mask bring a goat") and the theme is "plotting to bring about a one world government," then getting tapped by a secret society should be high on your to-do list. Shrouded in mystery and usually having more money than morality, these bastions of privilege are independent from the schools where they are located, and many own the buildings where they meet, so the only limit to their "good works" are Hegel's dialectic and the liquidity of the global heroin market.

Do Your Homework

Many secret societies don't even reveal their real names and activities until after you've joined, so make sure you at least get a hint of what the society is about, be it burning kittens to starting forest fires, otherwise you'll join the cool and cryptically named ZZ Top and 77 Society, only to run into fourteen burly seniors wearing fake beards and sombreros tugging on their chorizos and staring fixedly at your Adam's apple.

Similarly, before joining the Secret Owl Society, make sure it isn't a worldwide forum for people interested in owls.

Many only admit 15 or 16 in a year, usually from influential families and those of former members. So, if you were born a nobody, you'll have to find another route to world domination.

Ritual

Try to join a society that keeps the ritual to a minimum, because after the novelty has worn off, all those hand gestures and lying naked in a coffin detailing your sexual exploits can become very tiresome.

What's in a Name?

Most of these societies follow the tradition set by Skull and Bones, and have two parts to their name. However, this means that they run the risk of sounding like quaint British biker pubs.

Tapping

On Tap Day stand in the quad with all the other junior hope-fuls. If you feel a tap on your shoulder, walk purposefully up to your dorm room and await further instructions. There, in private, you will be given the choice of accepting or rejecting an offer of membership. If you don't feel a tap—don't despair: It may simply be an indication that you're at MIT instead of Yale.

100. Run a Wet T-shirt Competition

Wet T-shirt competitions are sexy, sexist, and lots of fun. When H_2O and gazungas get together the results are always spectacular.

Find a Venue

You'll attract more people to your event (and more hot chicks prepared to get their tits soaked) if you approach a local bar and ask them to host it. They may even agree to give a free drink to each ticket holder, since they increase their take behind the bar.

Set a Date

If you plan to make this a regular event, keep the same day every week, or month, or whatever, so people know that Friday night is hooters night. The best time is late evening, around midnight, when plenty of alcohol has been consumed and people are feeling less inhibited.

Promote the Event

Charge a participation fee, sell tickets, hand out special-offer flyers, and put up a generous cash prize for first, second, and third place.

Prevent Lawsuits

All contestants must show picture ID proving that they are legally old enough to take part, and get them to sign an entry form which acknowledges their age, and absolving you of liability if they get injured or if photos or videos of them appear on the Internet or anywhere else. Just in case don't let anyone in the audience take photos or video—and watch out for cell phones. Make sure the stage is covered with a rubber mat or some other non-slippery surface, so no one slips and sues you for their injuries. Also, make sure water doesn't get anywhere near the electronic devices, or you could have an electrocution injury, a fire, or a power outage.

Secure the Staging Area

Make sure you've got some big tough guys to protect the contestants and prevent anyone from jumping onto the stage. Make it clear to the audience at the start that they will be thrown out if they try to grope or harass the girls.

Judging

The winner is usually the person who gets the most applause and cheers from the audience, but you can formalize the event by having a panel of judges. See if you can get a celebrity to be one of the judges, to help draw a crowd. Invite the local radio DJ to be another judge, so he'll promote the event on his show. Make sure you're one of the judges, so you get the best view and maybe even a few telephone numbers afterwards.

101. Avoid Being Scammed by a Bartender

There are dozens of bartender scams. Here are six of the most common.

Short Changing

Counting your change is inconvenient, and bartenders know it. Always take a few seconds to count your change, and if you suspect the bartender is short changing you, make a point of doing it while he is watching, so he knows you're onto him and won't risk it again.

Top Shelf Switcheroo

You pay extra for a top-shelf drink, but instead of getting premium vodka, the bartender pours you a regular shot from one of the standard bottles and pockets the difference. Never order a top-shelf drink unless you can see the bartender pour your drink. You're most likely to get scammed like this in a joint with waitress service.

Fat Tab

Before you start a tab, check with the bartender to see if the drinks will be itemized at the end of the night. If not, pay a round at a time. Otherwise, come the end of the night when everyone is drunk and no one can remember how many drinks they had, you won't notice the few extra drinks that have made their way onto your bill.

Cost Jumping

The bartender charges different prices to different customers for the same drink. If regulars are getting their drinks cheaper than you, then your inflated prices may be subsidizing them because the bartender has to balance the books—otherwise his boss will know what he's been up to. If this happens to you, order a different kind of drink (the bartender won't be able to pull this scam on every type of drink, as straight drinks are easier to audit than those with a high spillage rate like beer). If that doesn't work, go somewhere else.

Drink Shortening

There are plenty of ways of shortening a drink, but the most extreme version is to give you no shot at all. Say you order a gin and tonic. All the bartender has to do to convince you that your drink has gin in it is to dip the rim into a saucer of gin, then add the ice, tonic, and pretend to pour the gin (keeping thumb over the spout). When you drink you'll taste and inhale the gin on the rim, but you'll have been scammed.

Chipped Bottle

If you're sold a drink in a chipped bottle, ask for another one. Not only are you risking cutting yourself or even swallowing glass (since the glass chip may have fallen inside the bottle), the bartender may already have shown it to the boss and had it marked down as waste, meaning that every penny you pay him is going into his pocket.

102. Pass a Drug Test

The best way to pass a drug test is not to take one in the first place, but if your college or employer puts you on the spot, there are a few ways for a dope head to escape detection.

Jell-O Drink

This trick works only for fat-soluble drugs such as marijuana, heroin, and PCP, which means that they get stored in your fat cells. You can also disguise fat soluble steroids this way, but not completely. Don't try this if you are diabetic.

1. Dissolve a whole packet of Jell-O into half a glass of water and shake well. Don't put the solution into the refrigerator as you don't want the Jell-O to set; you want to be able to drink it.

2. Drink three glasses of tap water, or as much as it takes you to pee once or twice before the test.

3. Fifteen minutes before the test, drink the Jell-O solution. This will flood your body with sugar, so your body won't have to metabolize the oil in your fat cells to create energy.

Other sample spiking or masking products will also work, such as Mary Jane Super Clean 13 (liquid soap), Urinaid (glutaraldehyde), Klear (nitrite), but the testers now test with these products too.

Dilute the Sample

If you have access to warm water, you can dilute the sample to reduce concentration of the drug. This will work for performance enhancing drugs such as creatine that naturally occur in the body, but not for recreational drugs which shouldn't be there in the first place. Most testing facilities are wise to this, so they dye toilet water, and block access to other sources of water.

Switch the Sample

Switch your sample with one belonging to someone else, or use synthetic urine from a laboratory supplier. These come in either concentrated liquid or powdered form—just add warm water (92 degrees) and hide in a tiny thermos flask until required. The powdered form is better because the liquid form has no smell.

Shave Your Hair

Drugs leave their signature in your hair for years afterwards (it reaches the hair follicles through the blood vessels), so shave your head, armpits, pubes, chest, and legs to a length of no longer than half an inch (one inch is the minimum length of hair required for successful testing). Bleaching or dying your hair will not disguise the drugs.

Saliva Test

If you are asked to provide a sample of saliva or other oral fluids, despite all your previous preparations, you are screwed.

103. Get a Fake Passport

Securing a fake passport in Europe is as easy as buying a rack of automatic weapons in a 7-Eleven back home. Approach anyone on the streets and ask for directions to the nearest fake ID provider. Even if they aren't personally involved in counterfeiting they are sure to know someone who is.

Quality Goods

Large numbers of forged passports are available on the streets of countries like England, flooding there in staggering quantities from passport "factories" in Eastern Europe and Nigeria. If you're looking for real quality, then head for Bulgaria, which as well as offering popular summer beaches and mountain ski resorts, produces some of the highest quality passport fakes in the world. Czech passports are well worth checking out too.

– Cheap and Realistic –

Whichever country you choose for fake citizenship, you'll find cheap and realistic products and you may even be able to negotiate a healthy discount when you buy in bulk. Hand over a wad of unmarked bills to a middle man (or woman), along with three recent passport photos, your height, age, and your new identity, and your documents will find their way to you quicker than you can say Shanghai Surprise. While we're on the subject of the Far East, Thailand has recently emerged as the world capital for fake passports tailored to the terrorist and criminal communities. However, don't bother going there, since up to 90 percent of the fakes are bound for Europe anyway. Fortunately even the British Home Office can't recognize a forgery even when it is under their nose. Recently a fake passport sent to them for verification was returned to an illegal immigrant without being detected.

Another option is to ask the International Red Cross to grant you a *laissez-passer* passport; rumor has it that their administrative procedures have little changed since they gave one to top Nazi Adolf Eichmann for his retirement in Argentina.

Once you've got your fake ID you can use it for identity theft, age deception, or organized crime. However, if you want to reduce your risk of being detected, choose the country with the most shambolic border controls, which is . . . you guessed it, the UK. As long as you look smart and confident, and don't bring too many bags with you, you'll be welcomed with open borders. However, when you fly home be warned that the UK charges obscenely high Air Passenger Duty (APD). How else can the government claw back money lost to the black economy through inept security arrangements?

104. Join an Anti-Whaling Crew

The roar of the waves, the thrill of the catch; the air is thick with the shrill cries of seamen as they face off against each other in a battle over the world's largest marine mammals. Roaming around the freezing seas of the North Pacific are vessels staffed with men armed with harpoons on the quest for a dwindling source of lipstick and protein. Chasing after them are speedy ships manned by animal-loving activists looking to put their boats between Ahab and Moby. Go on the high-seas adventure of your life and join the crew (that's protecting Moby, of course).

Do Your Research

If you think you've missed your vocation but don't know where to begin, you're never too old to start saving whales. However, as any career counselor will tell you, you'll need to do your research. So, if you haven't seen *The Perfect Storm* or *Free Willy* before, rent them on DVD pronto. You need to know what you're getting into when it comes to dangerous sailing conditions, and having a little boy's spirit to save a whale.

Understand Your Enemies

The majority of whaling crews hail from Japan. However, contrary to popular belief, the Japanese attitude to hunting isn't as profligate as it first appears. It was the Norwegians who introduced whale killing on a biblical scale at a time when Japanese fishermen regarded whales as gods of the seas, albeit tasty ones.

An international moratorium on whale hunting has been in force since 1986, but Japan is allowed to kill around a thousand whales each year for research purposes. They don't want to kill Willy to eat him. They just want to kill him, cut him up into a thousand little pieces, and study him.

Understand Your Crew

If you are serious about heading out on open water to stop the slaughter of the ocean's gentle giants, look into joining the ranks of the Sea Shepherd Conservation Society. This non-profit sails out of Washington state as well as Melbourne, Australia, and was featured on the Animal Planet's *Whale Wars*.

The goal of Sea Shepherd is to protect endangered marine mammals like whales, dolphins, and seals. They go about their conservation efforts by conducting non-violent assaults on whaling boats, both at sea and on the docks. A favored tactic is "stink-bombing" the ships with butyric acid, which they like to describe as "basically rancid butter." So pack up those sticks of butter that have been sitting in the back of your fridge since '98 and go out and eighty-six those whalers.

105. Get Bumped Up to First Class

On an airplane the comfort gap between First Class and coach is enough to make you chew your polyester seat with envy: delicious foods, personal HD TV, more leg room than the Boston Celtics bench, plus you avoid lowlifes like you. There are health benefits too: on a long haul flight you'll need some quality sleep and want to reduce the risk of getting a deep vein thrombosis. So how do you get bumped up to First?

1. **Getting anything for nothing is always a matter of psychology and how you deal with human beings, because they sit between you and comfort.** First of all, you've got to look like you belong in First Class, so wear a suit, look clean and well-groomed, and act confident (but not brash). The other flyers have paid a lot of money to avoid scruffy backpackers, children, and other forms of pond life, so you won't stand a chance of upgrading if you look like you belong with the sweating masses.

2. If you have frequent flyer status then you will have priority over other coach-class customers. Failing this, make sure you look like a seasoned traveler rather than a newbie looking for a freebie.

3. Pick the right moment. Usually if there are some upgrades happening, they are awarded to those frequent flyers who checked in first, but equally, if you check in last the ticket counter agent will have a better idea of how many free First Class seats are available or unclaimed.

4. If the flight is oversold, offer to be bumped on to the next flight. If the airline can't get you on another flight within an hour, you'll get a free ride. And they will look favorably on you if any First Class seats come up for grabs.

5. When booking explain that you are a famous travel writer, and ask for an OSI code to be added to your record. At the check-in hold your doctored copy of an influential travel guide (with your name prominently displayed on the spine and front cover), and explain your requirements. Most airlines will bend over backwards to ensure you give them a favorable report.

6. Don't use the word "upgrade." It's too pushy and clumsy. Be a little more sophisticated by enquiring if you can have a seat close to the front, or one with more leg room.

7. Cause a problem with your seat. Damage the safety belt, smear excrement on the food shelf, or crush some peanuts on your seat and then explain to the flight attendant that you are allergic to nuts and will go into anaphylactic shock unless you are moved to a First Class seat where you can be absolutely certain that you won't be exposed to any more nut-based hazards. If they don't believe you, show them your adrenalin pump and tracheotomy scar (this requires prior preparation).

8. You can also get moved if you have a legitimate complaint against a neighboring passenger. If he is a man, complain that he keeps pressing himself against you and staring at your genitals.

If all else fails, fake your own death shortly after take off. It is standard practice for corpses to be moved to First Class where there is more space, but choose your airline carefully: some carriers such as Singapore Airlines have introduced "corpse cupboards" to stow the recently deceased, so you might find yourself being unceremoniously stuffed into one of the cabin crew's personal lockers.

106. Become a Snake Charmer

What about snake charming doesn't sound like a great idea? Sitting inches away from a poisonous snake, taunting it with obnoxious flute music, having it rise into striking position . . . it sounds awesome! If you're interested in learning the tricks of the trade, you should head over to India where the modern concept of snake charming originated.

What's the Charm?

Once seen as a national treasure—snake charmers were flown around the world to promote tourism to India—the practice is now technically outlawed; however, you can still find practitioners throughout the country, playing their instruments and making their serpents wiggle and rise from their baskets.

Snake charmers set up shop like other types of street performers. They try and find a heavily trafficked area and claim a spot where they can set their basket and begin playing their *been* or *pungi*, the flute-like instrument favored by charmers. As the charmers play their music, the snake—usually a cobra or viper—rises from the basket and waves in the air as if entranced by the music. In actuality, the snake cannot hear the music, but can feel the vibrations. Also, it is not hypnotized; it is just getting into a defensive position in order to strike.

Where to Begin

First things first, if you want to be a snake charmer, you need a snake. You could go out in the Indian wild and try your luck at capturing a cobra. Chances are you will wind up getting bitten. Therefore, you should head to a local gift store and purchase the realest looking, fake snake that you can find. Trust us, this is much safer.

Snake in the Grass

Seeing as how your fake snake will not be reacting to the vibrations put out by your flute, you are going to need to get creative. After you purchase an authentic Indian basket, you will need to buy some extra-fine fishing line. Next, find a place to set up your scam that has some sort of overhang. A street light or building's eave should work. You need to tie the line around your snake's head, loop it over the overhang, and tie it around your flute. Once you take the top off your basket, begin playing your flute, twisting the instrument clockwise as you play. This will reel the line around the flute and raise your snake. Be sure to move the flute around as it will not only make your snake "dance" but it will distract your onlookers. When the snake reaches its peak height, begin twisting the flute counter-clockwise in order to put your snake to bed.

107. Street Race in Malaysia

Street racing is illegal in Malaysia, but that doesn't stop an estimated 200,000 young men from cruising the streets most evenings in their modified cars or sucky little motorcycles in search of an adrenalin rush. If you want to join the scene, buy a scooter or an old Malaysian banger, and see how quickly you can wedge yourself under a truck.

Mat Rempit

If you race your car or crappy little *kapcai* (scooter) on the street, you are known as *Mat Rempit* in Malay. The root of the term lies in the combination of the expression "ramp the throttle" and the noise made by a two-stroke engine. To impress your girlfriend, you should spend most of your free time performing pointless modifications on your vehicle to squeeze a bit more power from your pathetic piece of junk, and make the exhaust sound less like a hairdryer.

Mat Rempit like to show off (and distinguish themselves from pizza delivery boys) by performing stunts such as the "superman" (head and shoulders at handlebar height, body flat, and one leg cocked on the back of the seat); "scorpion" (stand on the seat with one leg during a wheelie); "sailboat" (stand on the seat and steer with the feet); and "*wikang*" (front wheelie). These efforts are based on the principle that the more stupid the stunt, the more attention is diverted away from your ridiculous bike.

Cilok Racing

Cilok is racing a scooter while weaving in an out of moving and stationery traffic (optional: then posting a video on You-Tube of you reaching the speed limit while going downhill with a tailwind).

Car Racing

Most racers are low-paid or unemployed, so they don't have much money to spend on their cars. Most drive something home-grown or Japanese like a boxy first-generation Proton Douche-bag, a small hatchback Daihatsu R-Tard, or a fifteen-year-old Nissan Pantyliner.

Routes

Recently the police have clamped down on illegal racing, but on weekend nights you'll still find a meet in many of the city centers (Kuala Lumpur, Selangor, Johor Bahru), or check out the drift racing on hill roads such as Bukit Tinggi or Teluk Bahang in Penang. Even watching street races is illegal, so if the police arrive hit the gas and speed away as quickly as your 50cc engine will allow.

108. Break Into a Panda Reserve

There are only an estimated 1,000 giant pandas left in the wild, and they are among the most threatened large mammals in the world. So you really don't have the time to wait for the red tape to clear on your request to visit a panda reserve. By the time all your paperwork is processed, you are approved, and you get to the top of the waiting list, pandas may have gone the way of the dodo.

Where Have All the Pandas Gone?

Besides the fact that humans slaughtered pandas for thousands of years, the black-and-white bears really aren't doing much to help their species. First, despite the fact that they are really carnivores, modern pandas have become such fussy eaters that they only eat bamboo shoots, and not any old shoots either—only one specific type. Also, their digestive system, which is crying out for flesh, can only digest about two percent of the bamboo, and the rest of it passes through. So besides starving themselves, they don't really have any energy to waste having sex.

On the topic of reproduction, the male has an unfeasibly small penis, while the female has a gargantuan vulva, so they aren't well matched. Also, the females are so stupid that the first time they give birth they beat the living crap out of their offspring because they have never seen a baby panda before. Truly, if they didn't look so cute, they'd have been allowed to die out decades ago.

Panda Reserves

To see a panda in the wild, you will need to travel to China. The Chinese government, along with various wildlife organizations, has set up panda reserves in an attempt to try and save the species. However, access to these areas is extremely limited and the reserves are well patrolled.

If you are willing to risk it all though, your best bet is to head to the Sichuan Giant Panda Sanctuaries in the southwest Sichuan province of China. The Sanctuaries are made up of seven nature reserves and nine scenic parks, with the Wolong National Nature Reserve housing 150 pandas. The large panda population makes this your best option. A stream runs through the Wolong Valley where the reserve is located. Try and find an entry point to the stream that lies outside the reserve's watchful eye. Under the cover of darkness, paddle down the stream and into the reserve.

Alternatives

Go to the zoo. The zoos in San Diego, Atlanta, and Washington, D.C. all have pandas. Slip the security guard a hundred bucks and may be he'll let you sleep next to the glass.

109. Be a Drug Mule

Being a drug runner isn't as easy as it was during the '60s, when criminals were way ahead of the game and airport surveillance was in its infancy. Now with a very real prospect of getting caught, you've got to weigh your fee against the possibility of spending twenty years rotting in a foreign jail, with cockroaches nesting in your ears, and a cellmate who wants to re-enact some of the missing scenes from *Milk*.

Body Packing

Drug mules who carry merchandise inside their own bodies (stomach, rectum, vagina, etc.) are called "body packers"; "swallowers," well . . . swallow. It's less risky than keeping it in your carry-on in terms of getting caught (although your body may still be X-rayed by airport security), but potentially much more dangerous to your health. Don't swallow hashish as the fee won't compensate for the risk. You can carry around two pounds of Class A drugs in your stomach. The old-fashioned method is to fill condoms to make little pellets, and then swallow them. Later, you use laxatives like diphenoxylate or loperamide to get them to come out quickly. Enemas are also recommended if you've shoved any drugs up your ass.

The dangers are considerable: if you suddenly develop acute anxiety, dilated pupils, a rapid heartbeat, and can't stop sweating, the condom has split and is leaking inside you. You have two choices: check yourself into the ER where you will be treated for a drug overdose, and then arrested (and your handlers will probably want to kill you), or sweat it out alone and pray you don't die from an overdose. Just remember, sometimes your handlers won't wait for you to pass the drugs out naturally—they will kill and cut you open.

If everything goes according to plan, you'll be paid a fee related to the number of pellets you have swallowed—about $8,000 per kilo maximum—plus your air fare and hotel expenses. The cartel will sell the drugs for five or six times this price and the street value in a city like New York could be forty times your cut.

Know Your Back Story

If you're supposed to be on vacation, have vacation plans, know where you are going to stay, and have the right amount of luggage. Dress appropriately (i.e. don't be the only person wearing casual clothes on a mid-afternoon flight full of suited business travelers). Don't board or disembark from the plane first or last (this is what drug mules usually do). Don't be overly cooperative with customs officials.

Smuggling Routes

Smuggling around Europe or from Panama into the United States is preferable to Asia, where many countries have mandatory death penalties for anyone caught with even the smallest amounts of drugs. For example, in Singapore the death sentence is mandatory for trafficking in more than 15 grams of heroin, 30 grams of cocaine, or 500 grams of cannabis, and your family won't even be notified that you've been hung until after your death. Avoid China, Thailand, Brazil, India, and Saudi Arabia as well—you don't even want to go to prison in these countries, let alone die. The best place to make your runs are the Scandinavian countries where, if you get caught, you'll be sent to a humane facility where you will be fed on wild pheasant and caviar and can get yourself a college education.

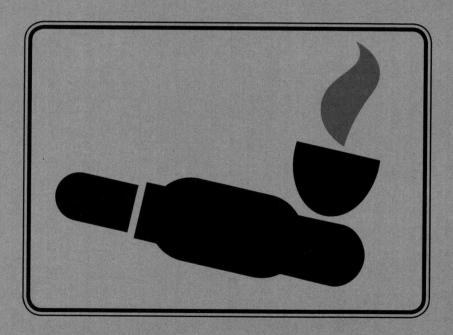

110. Land a Plane in Red Square

At around 7.00 P.M. on May 28, 1987, nineteen-year-old German political activist Mathias Rust landed a light aircraft on a bridge next to St. Basil's Cathedral, and then taxied to within 100 yards of Red Square. If you want to recreate Rust's historic feat, you'll need an extraordinary amount of luck, just like him. Air defense systems are more sophisticated than twenty years ago, and post-9/11, rogue aircrafts are certain to be shot down. But what the hell: here's how to follow his route in five easy steps:

1. Rent a plane in Hamburg, Germany. Rust rented a Reims Cessna F172—a four-seat, single-engine, fixed-wing plane, and the most successful mass produced light aircraft in history. Good choice. Other options include the Piper PA-28 Cherokee, the Grumman American AA-5 series, or the Diamond DA40 (which is the most attractive ride—the others look a bit boxy).

2. In the morning, fly to Finland and refuel at Helsinki-Malmi Airport. Ask air traffic control for clearance to fly to Stockholm in Sweden, but instead, turn off all your communication equipment and head east.

3. At some point along your route, air traffic control may think you've crashed and will go about starting a search and rescue mission. This is costly; Rust was charged $100,000 for his.

4. Cross the Baltic coastline in Estonia and then turn towards Moscow. By now the Russian military should have assigned you a combat number, and several surface-to-air missile (SAM) divisions start have you in their sights. Rust was lucky that permission to engage was withheld. Post-9/11 you won't be.

5. If by a miracle you are still alive, look out for interceptor planes. If they don't shoot you down, land near Staraya Russa, an old Russian town fifty miles south of Veliky Novgorod. Change your clothes and eat some sandwiches, and then make the final push to Moscow. Pray that the Central Air Defence System has been turned off for maintenance, and you should reach Red Square by early evening. You can try landing in the Square, but you'll kill lots of pedestrians.

Do Your Time

Rust was sentenced to four years in a Soviet labor camp, but he actually served only 432 days in an interrogation prison because the KGB couldn't guarantee his safety. He was locked up in a thirteen square-yard cell for twenty-two hours each day and it hit him "so hard—much harder than I had thought." However, you'll be lucky to reach Step 4, so anything else is a bonus.

111. Swim with Sharks

There are few killers more efficient than the great white shark, a carnage machine that grows up to twenty feet long and 5,000 lbs in weight, with teeth sharper than a scalpel blade. It is at the top of its food chain, so the moment you get into the water with one you become prey. In the last fifteen years, there have been approximately 900 shark attacks of which 100 have been fatal. If you want to swim with sharks and survive, pay attention:

1. Florida has the highest incidence of shark attacks in the world, followed by Australia, South Africa, Brazil, and Hawaii.

2. Some species of shark come inshore to feed at dawn, dusk, and during the night, so avoid the water at these times in high-risk areas.

3. Sharks are attracted to splashing and activity in the water, so try to swim smoothly and keep pets and children out of the water, as they are always splashing around. Surfing appears to be the biggest risk factor; you are twice as likely to be attacked while surfing than while diving. The reason for this is that the activity on the surface of the water attracts the sharks.

4. Don't swim with an open wound. Sharks can detect blood and other bodily fluids in minute concentrations. If you are bleeding or have an open wound, stay out of the water, and don't pee in your wetsuit when there are sharks around.

5. A shark like a great white will take an exploratory nibble then come back for the kill. If you can flee after the first nibble, you will escape with your life.

6. A shark's eyesight can pick out contrast well, so avoid wearing high contract clothing, or shiny objects such as jewelry.

7. Stay away from people who are fishing, and don't swim if you've recently handled dead fish or other dead animals like if you've been gutting fish.

8. Don't swim alone. If you get attacked, your friends can pick up the pieces and bring them to shore.

112. Lie Effectively

There are lots of ways to spin untruths, but many people get caught lying all the time. Here are ten tips to make you a better liar.

1. Relax. Nervous people seem like they're lying even when they're not. If you want someone to believe your lie, it's more about how you say it than what you say.

2. Tell people what they want to hear. People are more likely to believe a lie if you tell them what they would rather hear from you. It's even better if it's what they expect to hear.

3. Keep close to the facts. The fewer points at which you deviate from the truth, the easier it is to keep your story straight.

4. If you can't go small, go big. If there are any outrageous truths you can toss into your lie, use them. Give your audience something they can't believe to be true and then prove it's so. This makes it easier for a listener to swallow the rest of the story.

5. Look people in the eye. Liars tend to evade direct eye contact.

6. Deny, deny, deny. Put the burden of proof on those who call you a liar. Make them prove their accusations. It's a lot harder to do than most people think.

7. Switch the subject. If someone manages to prove you lied about something, change the course of the conversation to something else. State that the lie is trivial, the product of a mistake rather than malice, and that it's beside the (new) point anyhow.

8. Suffer from memory loss. If the event you need to lie about is further in the past than a few hours back, repeat this phrase: "I can't recall." It worked for the Gipper and a good chunk of the Bush administration. It can work for you.

9. Split hairs. Play with the definitions of words. Bill Clinton raised such prevarication to an art form when arguing about "what the meaning of the word 'is' is." 10. Establish an alibi. Get your friends to lie for you. This is especially effective if you're all involved in the same lie and are lying for each other. Chances that any of you will crack drop dramatically.

113. Stow Away on Board a Ship

A stowaway is anyone who hides on a train, bus, plane, ship, or bicycle in the hope of getting something for nothing, or moving from one country to another illegally. As most sensible people know, you get what you pay for, and when you become a stowaway, you expose yourself to considerable danger and discomfort. There are also serious legal consequences if you are discovered, especially on a plane. If you get caught you will most likely be treated as a terrorist and get hauled off to Cuba for some heavy-duty waterboarding.

Freight with Danger

Each form of transport comes with its own risks. Every year lots of people are injured trying to jump off moving trains, while airplane stowaways are often found frozen to death inside the landing gear. The major hazard for ship stowaways is choosing the wrong hold and being crushed by millions of tons of cargo, or being unprepared for the length of the trip. Be ready for many weeks at sea; be sure to have adequate supplies of food and water you will be dead within a few days. That said, there is a certain romantic appeal to placing your fate in the hands of a crew of jolly jack tars as they sail their trade through the high seas.

The safest vessel on which to hitch a lift is a container ship, as they have low levels of security and more places to hide, especially empty containers. The port and starboard service tunnels which run below decks are good places to board.

Longshoremen

Many stowaways have successfully posed as dock laborers by dressing up like Marlon Brando in *On the Waterfront*. If you don't own a leather jacket, then a hard hat, jeans, and an orange visibility jacket will suffice. When lifting, always bend your knees and keep your back straight, otherwise everyone will quickly spot an impostor. Also, learn a few knots, because you may be asked to throw together a Square Knot Bracelet to prove your credentials. Bone up on a few nautical terms before your trip, so that if you are challenged you can slap your thigh and speak authentically: "Arr, listen close me hearty, I be no landlubber by the powers, as ye soon shall see mateys, or ye can call me a scurvy dog!" As the gulls wheel overhead, hand them back the knotted rope with a toothless grin and, with a glint in your good eye, offer to buy them a quart of grog.

114. Be a Sex Tourist

The international tourism industry is booming and the sex industry is ever burgeoning as air travel becomes cheaper and cheaper. If you want to spend your vacation dollars wisely, then you can do no better than boost the economy of a third world country. Instead of offering hand-outs, you'll be paying for a service which gives its impoverished participants dignity and the prospect of a better life.

Saving Lives

It goes without saying that the best place to exploit people for sex is in poor countries where you can offer financial incentives in exchange for tricks. When someone is on the bread line, not only does your money help to boost the economy, it also literally saves lives. The most significant societal factor that pushes people into prostitution is poverty, so the only responsible thing is for the more fortunate among us to do whatever we can to alleviate their suffering. Poverty also correlates with illiteracy, so you can have the added satisfaction of knowing that you are helping to educate as well.

Better the Devil You Know

Oftentimes, women are lured to the cities with hopes of finding work. They rely on your money when those jobs fail to materialize. Many prostitutes live in constant fear of being beaten up by clients or by pimps, or being arrested by the police. At least you know that when you show them a littlekindness and financial assistance, it's one less reason for them to take risks or feel depressed.

Where to Go

Now that we've made the case for sex tourism, we just have to point you in the right direction. Between 2 and 14 percent of the gross domestic product of Indonesia, Malaysia, the Philippines, and Thailand comes from sex tourism, but if you are worried about your carbon footprint when you fly half way around the world to avoid the laws in your own country, then go to closer-to-home locations like Mexico and Central America, which have much to satisfy the libido of the wary traveler.

115. Waterboard a Terrorist

There's been a lot of debate about whether or not certain practices the U.S. Government has approved for use in the War on Terror constitute torture. The most contentious of these is water-boarding, originally known as the Chinese water torture. This causes a victim to feel like he's drowning but in theory does no direct physical harm—other than potentially causing a stroke, heart attack, or other catastrophe from the stress.

The Catholic Church apparently used waterboarding in the Spanish Inquisition, and it's been a favorite interrogation tool ever since, used by groups ranging from the Gestapo to the Khmer Rouge. Today, members of the U.S. special forces undergo waterboarding as part of their survival school training.

Here's how it's done.

1. Strap the victim down on his back. Traditionally, this involves immobilizing him on a board (thus the name of the technique), but anything that holds him down should do.

2. Raise the victim's feet so they are higher than the head.

3. Cover the victim's face or stuff a rag into his mouth. You can use a cloth for this, although some have used cling wrap with a hole pierced for the mouth.

4. Pour water over the victim's face.

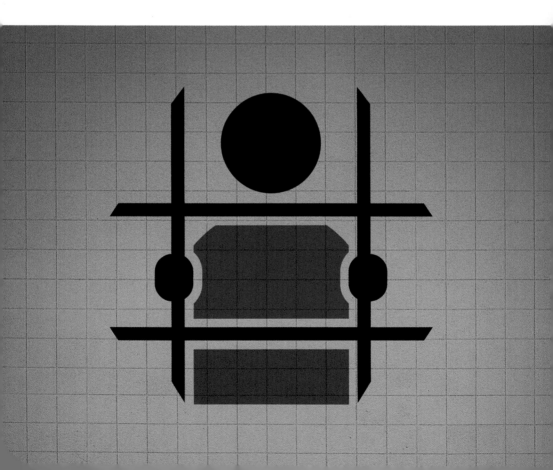

How It Works

The water induces the gag reflex and causes the victim to feel like he is drowning. Reportedly even CIA agents cannot endure this for longer than 15 seconds.

How to Get Away with It

If you're a private citizen and get caught doing this, the police will want to have a long chat with you, followed by a long visit in the appropriate lock-up. If you're part of the CIA or the U.S. military, you may find that your superiors have granted you limited permission to use this technique, despite the fact that U.S. soldiers and officers faced court-martial charges for doing so in both the Vietnam and Spanish-American Wars.

116. Cheat at Gambling

There are many different ways to cheat at gambling, but the idea behind them all is the same: to take the money of the other players without letting them know you're cheating. If you want to rob someone, it's simpler to just mug him—and possibly more honest. .

There are three main ways to cheat at gambling.

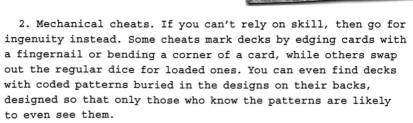

1. Skilled cheats. This is the classic kind of cheating you see in all sorts of films and shows. It involves things like palming cards, controlled rolling, dealing from the bottom of the deck, or having the infamous ace up your sleeve. This is a difficult way to cheat, as it requires a lot of practice. Also those who perform such tricks usually know how to spot them.

2. Mechanical cheats. If you can't rely on skill, then go for ingenuity instead. Some cheats mark decks by edging cards with a fingernail or bending a corner of a card, while others swap out the regular dice for loaded ones. You can even find decks with coded patterns buried in the designs on their backs, designed so that only those who know the patterns are likely to even see them.

3. Teamwork. Most card games are built on the premise that each player only knows the content of his own hand. Players who somehow share information can turn the odds in their favor. This is why table talk is usually discouraged.

Casinos Can Cheat Too

If any player can cheat, there's little (outside of gambling regulators and savvy players) to keep casinos from doing so too. In the case of large casinos in big cities like Las Vegas, there's the threat of losing a reputation as an honest house too, but for smaller operations that's less of a disincentive.

Some such places can use a shoe (a device used in a casino to hold several decks of cards shuffled together) rigged to keep the top card (usually a face card) in place until the dealer wants it. Others might have a craps table with a foot-activated electromagnet built into the base. Couple this with a set of dice with iron filings mixed into the paint on one face of each die, and you have a system that's hard to spot and impossible to beat.

117. Get Out of Handcuffs

If you happen to find yourself bound with your hands behind your back, you're likely in a heap of trouble. If you've been arrested by the police, your best bet is to leave the handcuffs on. Removing them could be construed as resisting arrest or an attempt to escape, both of which are serious charges to add on to whatever you were arrested for in the first place.

If you have some other good reason to remove handcuffs, though, here's how.

Pick It

The locks on most handcuffs are fairly simple. This is one reason your hands are usually placed behind your back when you're cuffed. It's hard to undo a lock you can't see, even if you happen to somehow have a key.

Assuming you don't have a key, look for a piece of wire with which you can fashion a crude lockpick. A bobby pin works well for this, once you strip off the plastic bits on the end. In a pinch (like what you're probably in), you can use a paperclip.

Bend the end of the wire at a right angle about a quarter inch from its end. Then, about halfway back to the top, bend it back in the original direction. Push this into the lock. Use the bend to shove down the little post in the center of the lock, then twist your pick around until the lock opens.

Shim It

Handcuffs resize automatically to fit their captives by means of serrated teeth that go through a one-way ratchet. If you have a thin, stiff piece of wire—say the tip of a safety pin—you may be able to shim the ratchet open. To do this, slip this between the teeth and the ratchet. If done correctly, the cuffs should easily pull off your wrists.

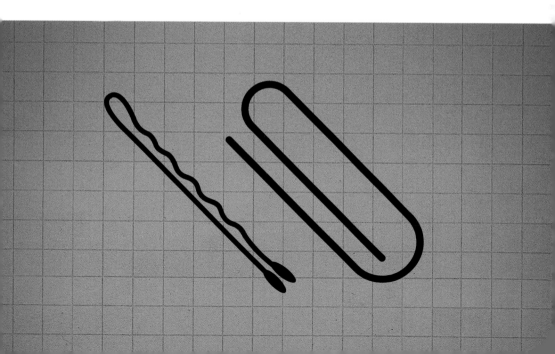

— Slip Free —

If you have nothing from which you can fashion a pick or a shim, you can try to get free the old-fashioned way and just slip your wrists out of the cuffs. If they've been put on properly, this can be a difficult trick, and even trying it can cost you some skin around your wrists.

If possible, rub lubricant of some kind on your skin and the cuffs to help you slip free. Petroleum jelly is brilliant for this, but any kind of liquid—from spit to plain water—can help.

118. Start Your Own Fraternity

Joining these elite social groups to facilitate wild partying and lots of sex (and if their PR is to be believed, plenty of charitable works) holds a certain attraction (apart from the charity part). Who wouldn't want to gain a band of brothers who will stand by you for life, or simply drag you to the john so you can barf? However, pledging is a big pain in the ass, the dues are expensive, the time commitment is prohibitive, and once you've finished pledging, you'll probably realize you have little in common with most of the other brothers after all. There is a cheaper and more empowering alternative: Start your own.

Decide What You Stand For

Write down about ten goals or ideals to which your organization should aspire. Don't sweat it if you struggle to reach ten—even the Founding Fathers were only able to think of three self-evident truths. Don't worry if most of them are about keggers and getting laid, but remember to add a few worthy aspirations about being an asset to campus life, so when you ask for the Dean's approval you don't look like a members-only boning club.

Name It

   Devise a short motto that expresses your philosophy, and then write the initial letters of each word in Greek. Keep it brief because T-shirt logo printers charge by the letter. Some mottos like "Ethanol" or "Θα σου πιω το αίμα" (I will drink your blood) don't need any embellishment.

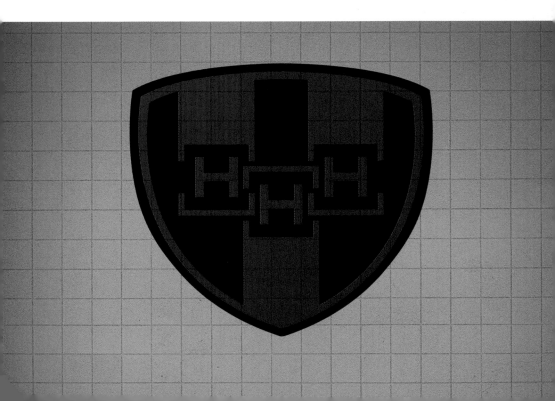

Collect Your Dues

One of the downsides of belonging to a fraternity is the
dues, which can range from $300—$1500 a semester, about half of
which goes to the national headquarters. No wonder they want to
get pledges. But if you start your own, you ARE the headquarters—you're the top of the whole stinking pyramid. Even if your
fraternity is just you and your rich gullible roomie, you get
to keep all the money, so long as you spend a nominal amount on
ritual props, fake blood, goats, past exam papers, books, ban-
ners, and other necessities.

Get Recognition from the Pan-Hellenic Council

After you've taken part in some campus events, approach the
Pan-Hellenic council and ask if you can join. Don't worry if
they threaten to ban you from campus—bribe them with your
first semester's dues and everything you make above that is
clear profit.

119. Get Served Underage

A bar can lose its licence if it is caught letting in or serving underagers, so the stakes are high. Whatever scam you pull to get past security, dress appropriately, look confident, and make good eye contact. Many 18+ clubs draw an X on your hand if you are underage, so before you go out cover your hand with clear glue. This way you can peel off the X in the bathroom. If that won't work, try these tricks before shelling out $100 for a fake ID.

Underage ID

If it's busy, sometimes just holding your underage ID ready and visible is enough to get you waved through.

Smoke Break

Pretend you've already been inside and you stepped out for a smoke or some fresh air—it's lame, but has been known to work.

VIP Status

If someone you're with who is of legal age can get a VIP upgrade (maybe they know the bar owner), there's a chance the bouncers will wave through your whole party without checking everyone's IDs.

Fake Wristbands

Colored wristbands are a common form of age identification in clubs, and they can easily be faked by either buying a set of bands off the Internet, or carrying your own collection of ¾-inch thick paper tape in a variety of colors. The most common colors are neon pink, neon yellow, neon green, neon orange, and white, but you'll also need a range of pastels.

Dragged from Work

Tell the doorman you just finished work and got dragged straight here by your hot boss (it helps if she's over 21), and didn't have time to go home to get your ID.

The Haley Joel Osment Method

If you have a friend who looks really young (about twelve) but is actually twenty-two, he will always get stopped first. The bouncers will spend lots of time scoping his ID, and they will ask lots of questions; after that, if the line is stacking up behind, they will probably wave the rest of you through.

Use the Dress Code

Break the dress code so you are refused entry. Explain that you live very close, and can run home to change if they'll let you skip the line when you get back. If the bouncer agrees, it's possible that when you return he'll remember you and let you in without checking your ID.

Fake Ticket

It's easy to get served at a ticket-only event. You just need to worry about getting in. You can fake a ticket by scanning a real ticket and printing your own copy. (You can even buy special scissors to cut perforations.) This probably won't work though if the tickets have serial numbers and the bouncers are crossing out names and numbers at the door.

Hand Stamp

Hand stamps are becoming more sophisticated, and many can only be seen under a black light, but the old-fashioned visible stamps can be faked using a sharpie marker, and then smudging it a bit. Or, you can find someone with a stamp and use a solvent to wet the ink, press their hand against yours, and transfer the mark.

Go Early, Stay Late

Many places only start checking IDs after 9 P.M., so you can go early to joints that serve food, eat, and then stick around as the over-21 crowd arrives.

Passport Scan

Take a color scan of your passport, change your age on Photoshop, print a copy on a high-quality printer, and tell the bouncer you lost your actual passport but the government office sent you a copy of the identification page.

Designated Driver

Explain that you are over 21 but you're not drinking tonight because you're the designated driver for a bunch of friends who are already inside.

120. Throw a Kicking Keg Party

A keg party is a great way to have all your stuff trashed and/or stolen, get college officials pissed at you, and facilitate the alcohol poisoning of strangers who crash your party. However, with a little planning, your keg party should be memorable, not one people want to forget.

Move Your Stuff to Secure Your Apartment

Lock all bedrooms and bathrooms that you want to keep people out of during the party, and carry the keys with you. Then, clear out the party areas to remove anything valuable or breakable. Also remove anything that could cause an injury or be used as a weapon. Don't be tempted to break your own rules during the party—once you let one couple get jiggy in a previously locked room you open the floodgates for getting your stuff trashed.

Rearrange the furniture to maximize space. If you've got a good carpet, cover it with a plastic tarp for protection. Black out all the windows and keep them shut (and locked, if possible) so you don't disturb the neighbors. Turn down the heating—the place will soon warm up when it's filled with a hundred sweating bodies.

Plenty of Trash Bags

Put a forty-gallon garbage can in every room, lined with a heavy-duty trash bag; if guests can't see a bin nearby you can bet they'll dump their crap on the floor.

Block Off the Kitchen

Put some crates in the doorway and set up a makeshift bar. That way you stop all the alchies from gathering in there and you can cut off the supply if the party starts to get out of control. Make sure you offer your guests plenty of water, so they can keep hydrated.

Sound System

Load up the evening's music on your iPod or computer, and keep it in a locked room so that drunk people don't mess around with it. It also means you can control the volume, because the louder the music the rowdier people get, so uncomfortably loud music is a recipe for brawling and blowing chunks.

Doorman

Have someone manning the door at all times to keep out punks and other troublemakers; choose someone who can not only handle themselves, but can also judge and communicate well with people to reduce the need for physical violence.

Police Radio

Get your hands on a police scanner so you can eavesdrop on their communications. If you get wind of an imminent bust, temporarily lock down your party: music off, no one enters or leaves until it's all clear.

The Keg Is King

Treat your keg or kegs with maximum respect, because if the beer sucks, so will your party. Put the keg in a spot where people will be able to access it easily. Place two sacks of ice in a large plastic tub, then sit the keg on top, pour ice and cold water down the sides, and on top of the keg. Only tap the keg after it has settled and cooled for an hour or two. You won't need to pump immediately after tapping because there will be plenty of carbonization already. People always over pump the keg at parties, and then lose lots of beer in foam. Pump the tap only when the beer flow begins to slow down.

121. Survive in the Australian Outback

G'day mate! There's a harsh reality to the friendly Australian people's backyard. The Outback is not a single place, but instead is the general term used by Aussies to refer to any part of the country that is not densely populated—which is virtually the whole thing. That means there's a lot of land to cover, tons of nature to see, and all sorts of trouble to find yourself in.

Get a start on your Outback adventure by renting a 4×4 in a northern city like Darwin and head south. The smart move would be to stick to the mapped highways and avoid going off-road. However, chances are you are not interested in smart moves. You will most likely find yourself completely lost. And that is when your real troubles will begin.

Outback Jackass

Besides the wide variety of snakes and spiders that are likely to deliver a poisonous bite when you go wandering outside your vehicle, the incredible heat of the Outback is a very big threat. There's a real danger to walking long distances while the sun is fully out as a bout of heatstroke will leave you incapacitated and easy pickings for a pack of wild dingoes. Unless you are left with no other option, stay in your 4x4 and sightsee from the driver's seat.

Crocodile Dundee-in-Training

Do NOT go near any bodies of water. No matter how hot you are and how tempting a dip in the river may seem, jumping in is an invitation to a feast where you are the main course. The Australian saltwater crocodile patrols the waters of northern Australia, with a typical male coming in at about fifteen feet long and weighing around 2,000 lbs. Just because you are away from the coastline does not mean you are safe from this territorial predator. The Australian saltwater crocodile is known to journey inland down freshwater rivers.

If you do happen to find yourself nose-to-snout with one of these beasts, you can try to defend yourself by holding the animal's snout closed. The animal's jaw has an extremely strong biting power, but a significantly weaker ability to open. Clamp the jaw down and hold on for a ride—it will likely be a short one.

Captain Those Kangaroos

A staple of the Australian Outback, the kangaroo is a dangerous adversary when it comes to road travel. The animal has been known to jump in front of cars when startled. And with a leaping speed of about 30 mph, it can cause quite the collision. Be careful as you travel down the roads and be mindful of the many kangaroo crossing signs you will see.

122. Traffic in Cultural Antiquities

The growth of tourism, the internationalization of the art market, and the 2003 invasion of Iraq mean that there has rarely been a better time for you to get involved in the trafficking of cultural antiquities.

Elgin Marbles

The benchmark by which all looters should measure themselves is of course, Thomas Bruce, 7th Earl of Elgin, who, in the early nineteenth century, removed the famous Elgin Marbles from the Parthenon in Greece, and hauled them back to Britain along with a piece of paper from the Ottoman Empire saying that he had won them fair and square in a game of Kerplunk. After a brief debate, Parliament decided that Elgin was a bloody good bloke and should be patted on the back for bagging such spiffy souvenirs. The British Museum bought them off him and they are now on display in the specially-built Duveen gallery (once a custom-made wing has been built to house your looted treasures, you know that they are staying put).

– Provenance –

As men with dark robes and gavels like to say, when it comes to stealing stuff from other countries, success depends upon provenance, provenance, *provenance*. If you don't have a paper trail proving that you acquired the artifacts legitimately, you may as well keep them under your bed at home because you won't be able to sell them on the international art market. Only kidding: there has always been a flourishing trade in stolen treasures, and just about every museum and auction house in the world is complicit.

– The Price of Democracy –

Be prepared to travel to places that other people are fleeing, namely war zones. Even though the wholesale looting of Iraq's museums and archaeological sites has been going on for five years, there is still plenty of stuff being dug out of the ground daily (some estimates are as high as 15,000 artifacts every day), and still no one is stopping it. However, you will have to fend off all the Iraqis who are plundering their own national heritage in the name of *zakat*, the Islamic principle that everything belongs to God and wealth is held by humans in trust. This makes it OK for them to sell looted goods to fund insurgency against coalition forces. In the words of the great political philosopher Donald Rumsfeld, "Democracy is messy."

123. Have Sex on a Beach

Making love on a beach is many people's fantasy, and as fantasies go, it is quite achievable. Just get yourself down to the nearest coastline with your partner and make like rabbits. The chance of getting caught, plus the sound of the waves lapping at your feet, with a huge red sun sinking below the horizon, is an appealing scenario. The reality will probably be otherwise—and is it really any different to screwing in the park or behind a dumpster? It's all in the mind. If you get intimate at the seaside, be prepared for three things to happen, (besides getting arrested):

1. You will be secretly filmed by someone hiding in the dunes, and your coupling will be available somewhere on the Internet by the end of the week. That is a certainty. Know that it will happen and live with the consequences. Choose your location carefully. And if you think making love in the water will be better, you'll get filmed by more than one person. Even if you think there's no way you could be spotted, you'll be wrong. Your actions will end up on a mainframe somewhere, even if it's the database of a Russian

satellite, or the live feed from a coastguard helicopter. Take a blanket to provide some cover.

2. Beaches are covered in sand. Now, you may be dimly aware of this fact on a superficial level, so let's spell it out again: S-A-N-D. Among the many properties enjoyed by granulated rock, the fact that it gets everywhere and there's nothing you can do about it, no matter how many towels you bring, is most important. This means that a certain amount of frictional discomfort is inevitable and you will spend days chasing sand out of the most intimate places.

3. The sex will not live up to your expectations, in the same way that the lesbian kiss in *Vicky Cristina Barcelona*, making love in front of an open fridge, and trying to recreate the butter scene from *Last Tango in Paris* were ultimately disappointments. It will be neither as good nor as bad as most people want to tell you it is! Keep your hopes low and you may be pleasantly surprised.

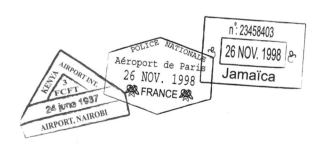

124. Start a Motorcycle Gang

Starting a bike gang isn't as easy as it used to be. A few decades ago, it was simply a matter of riding your hog down a dark alley and gathering together a collection of social misfits, sociopaths, and criminals. Today bike-riding crazies are a dying breed (or lifers) and harder to find than a horny panda, so you have to be more inventive to track them down.

Start a Fight

Walk into the roughest bar in town, and challenge the assembled company to a fight with the weapon of choice for the aspiring motorcycle gang member: the pool cue. Anyone who accepts your challenge can join, but not until you've spent half-an-hour trading blows and trashing the joint. This form of recruitment appears frequently in the movies—big hairy men beat the crap out of each other to earn mutual respect.

Squares Need Not Apply

If you live in a more upmarket neighborhood, instead of fighting, hand out application forms. Anyone who carries a pen on their person, or who actually fills in the form, is clearly unsuitable, whereas those who make a nihilistic gesture of rejection, such as setting your questionnaire on fire, or pulling down their pants and pissing on it, pass with honors.

Tattoos, beards, broken noses, scars, or a T-shirt slogan alluding to the ontological duality within biking culture (e.g. "Ride or die") are also highly desirable.

Naming Your Gang

Think of a name for your gang that implies menace but is also basic enough so that the illiterate members can paint it on their jackets. Also, everyone should adopt a road name. Decide whether you want your gang to be a weekend activity or a way of life on the wrong side of the law. If biking and brotherhood is your life calling, then technically you are what is known in biking circles as a One Percenter, and should wear a One Percenter patch (this is a diamond or rhombus shape). If even this is too conformist for you, then why not cut off your arms and live in a barrel. Seriously, when are you going to meet the world half way?

Stay Safe

In today's health-conscious society, it is reasonable to allow non-smokers to join, but don't compromise with road safety: make sure everyone knows their turn signals. There's a time and a place for pulling wheelies and burning out your back tire, but flagrant disregard of the Highway Code takes the rebel ethos a step too far.

125. Protect Against a Tiger Attack

If you are backpacking around India or Asia and you are running short on funds, you might want to consider skipping the expensive hotel or hostel and sleeping off the beaten path in the woods. However, opting to camp to save cash presents one big risk: tigers.

Odds in Your Favor

Tigers are an endangered species; only about 5,000 to 7,500 tigers are left in the wild. You will likely luck out and a hungry tiger will not wake you from your sleep. Instead, a poisonous snake will probably bite you. Sweet dreams!

Night Walker

If you do find yourself in tiger territory though, chances are you will be attacked in your sleep. Tigers are typically nocturnal hunters. With tigers coming in at about ten feet long and weighing approximately 400 to 570 lbs, you really don't stand a chance. Even if it isn't completely dark out, the tiger's stripes are perfect camouflage for the long grass you're probably settling down in.

The tiger will likely stalk your campsite in perfect silence before leaping out and pouncing on you. An adult tiger has an average horizontal leap of about fifteen feet. So you probably won't hear it pouncing until after it has its paws on your chest and is biting at your throat. At least it will be so quick you won't feel (most of) the pain.

Protect Your Campsite

A smart choice if you do make the stupid one to camp in the Asian wilderness is to fortify your site. Here are some suggestions:

Booby trap: dig a few ditches around your site and cover them up with some small branches and leaves. When the tiger circles your camp sizing you up, chances are it will fall into one of the hidden holes. (If it works in the movies, it has to in real life, right?)

Bird lime: spread a sticky mixture of mustard oil and latex around your site so that the tiger will step in the goo. When it tries to clean itself, it will transfer the stickiness onto its face. Dust, leaves, and other debris will now stick to the tiger's face and hamper its vision, making it unable to hunt.

Spikes: sharpen some bamboo rods into spikes and then drive them into the ground around your site, with the pointy ends sticking out. If you have enough time and energy to sharpen and build this type of barricade before nightfall, you should be safe—from tigers; this sort of thing won't stop those poisonous snakes.

126. Perform an Exorcism

If you are looking for a medical explanation for an individual with unnatural behavior, look no further than the seventeenth century's favorite diagnosis: demonic possession.

1. **Find yourself an exorcist and check his credentials.** In medieval and early modern times, the exorcist was a lower-ranking priest—one who had not yet successfully completed his Holy Orders. Today, exorcists are quite the opposite—they are senior and widely respected figures in the Roman Catholic Church. In either case, the exorcist can only face the devil head-on if he has the full authority of the Roman Catholic Church.

2. **The exorcist will select one or more assistants who may be other priests or laypersons, each of whom must swear to carry out the exorcist's commands and instructions immediately without question.** They must also make a full confession before the exorcism so as to be as free as possible from the guilt of sin that the devil will inevitably use against them.

3. Finally, you need to reach the conclusion that exorcism is the only means of saving the poor soul. The exorcist will need to place the possessed person in a room in which they are generally most comfortable and feel most secure, often their own bedroom.

4. The room is cleared of anything that could potentially be moved, hurled, or thrown: inexplicable telekinesis and flying objects are a real safety hazard.

5. Windows and doors must be sealed so as to contain the force of evil within as confined a space as possible.

6. Equipped with a crucifix, Holy Water, two candles, and a Bible, the exorcism begins. No one addresses the devil directly at any stage. The exorcism is a sacrament with a set pattern. The exorcist must adhere strictly to this if the devil is to be driven out. The process may last for days, and it continues without significant breaks until the devil is finally ousted.

127. Perform a Handbrake Turn

The handbrake turn—changing direction by 180 degrees within the width of a two-lane road in a few seconds—is an essential evasive driving technique. It is also known as the bootlegger's turn as it is thought to have been used (if not invented) by hillbilly moonshiners to escape from revenue agents.

The Bootlegger's/Handbrake Turn

It is much easier to perform this maneuver in a car that has an automatic transmission and a hand-operated emergency brake.

1. Reduce or increase your speed so that it is between 25 and 30 mph.

2. Take your foot off the gas and then turn the steering wheel about half a full turn, while simultaneously applying the emergency brake. If your car has a manual transmission, floor the clutch as well to keep the engine from stalling.

3. When the car is sideways, release the emergency brake, step on the gas, and straighten the steering wheel. With a manual transmission, let out the clutch as you apply the gas.

4. Speed away, but make sure you don't crash headlong into your baffled pursuers.

The bootlegger's turn punishes tires, so be sure to practice with your parent's car, a rental, or a stolen vehicle.

The Moonshiner's Turn

This is a reverse bootlegger's turn, which uses similar principles while the car is traveling in reverse. It is an effective way of escaping from a roadblock.

1. Accelerate in reverse to a speed of 25 to 30 mph.

2. Take your foot off the gas, and then turn the steering wheel all the way to the left as quickly as possible.

3. When the car is sideways, shift from reverse into a low gear, straighten the steering wheel, and hit the gas.

4. Speed away, while ducking to avoid the automatic gunfire that will by now be pelting your back windshield.

128. Make College Last Forever

If someone asking you, "So, what are you going to do after you graduate?" causes physical pain, you don't need a doctor to tell you have a Van Wilder complex. If you take enough drugs you can make time stop for a while, but there are other ways of staying in college forever, even after your parents decide to cut you adrift. Simply get industry fat cats to give you a truckload of backhanders to do biased research in key areas.

Kill Google

If your PhD thesis is called "Ways to make Google bend over and take it up the ass," Steve Ballmer will personally hand deliver a suitcase full of cash to your dorm every week. You'll have so much mullah stuffed under your mattress you'll be sleeping on the ceiling.

Peak Oil

Oil companies pay big bucks to academics to prop up the myth that the world is running out of the black stuff, so OPEC can restrict supply and hike up the price. Also required is research into even more far-fetched ways of getting it out of the ground, so when prices at the pumps stay high despite a slump in the global oil price, oil companies can say they are pumping all their profits into research and development (that's you buddy).

Global Warming

The big one—it's here, and we all knew it was coming, along with huge chunks of Antarctic ice and—get this—great gobs of cash heading into the pockets of anyone who can tell us whether we're going to flood, freeze, or fry, and how quickly it will happen. There are now so many hurricanes that you can get a grant just to count them. For thirty years the scientists have been telling us we're screwed, but it's only now that you can get mucho dinero to stay in college to study the global impact of reusing party toothpicks and mulching your lawn clippings.

Drug Companies

In 2002, the combined profits for the top ten drug companies in the *Fortune* 500 were more than for all the other 490 businesses put together. Wouldn't you like a slice of that rancid pie? Clinical studies sponsored by pharmaceutical companies are so routinely biased that weak data and marketing dressed up as research can keep you in Bud Lite and beer nuts for the rest of your days.

129. Elevator Surf

Elevator surfing does not require a wetsuit, you can't get attacked by sharks, you won't get knocked unconscious by a big wave, yet the practice of riding on top of an elevator, or jumping from one to another seems to have acquired a notoriety quite out of proportion to its danger. It's probably illegal, which means you need to stay alive and avoid detection.

Halt the Elevator Between Floors

Head to the elevators very early in the morning while the place is deserted. Board the elevator and press the "Stop" button while it is between floors. This may set off an alarm. If

so, press "Start" and postpone your attempt to another day. Next time you will need to stop the elevator between floors by prising open the internal doors to trip the safety stop mechanism. Once the elevator is held between two floors, open the internal doors and then undo the latch mechanism to open the external doors. Crawl out and then climb on top of the elevator. Alternatively you can open the exterior doors on the floor above and jump down or slide down the cable from there. If you can't get your hands on an elevator key, you'll have to simply force the external doors open from the outside.

Operate the Elevator

You should be able to control the elevator by using the control box on top of the elevator. The box will have several buttons and switches. Flick the one labeled "Inspection" or "Maintenance." This will disable the controls in the rest of the building, so that the elevator will only move under your manual control. Look for a "Run/Stop" switch, and flick it into the "Stop" position. Climb on top of the elevator and operate using the "Up/Down" switch. You may have to simultaneously press a safety switch to override the system. After you've had your fun, remember to put the elevator back into "Normal" mode.

Explore

Elevator surfing allows you to explore areas and even entire floors that might otherwise be off limits. At the top or bottom of the shaft, look for an entrance to the elevator mechanical room. That may lead you onto the roof or into a sub-basement. Or simply place the elevator into "Normal" mode and eavesdrop on people's conversations. Oh, and make sure you don't get your head cut off by the counterweight.

130. Swim with Piranhas

The jagged razor-sharp interlocking teeth of a piranha make it a fearsome predator (it can even bite through a steel fishing hook). Its name means "toothfish." A school of piranhas can strip a piece of meat to the bone in a matter of seconds, so if you have to cross piranha-infested waters it's best to take precautions to minimize the risk of being attacked.

Most species of piranha live in fresh water in South America, particularly in the Amazonian, Guianas, and Paraguayan river systems. They prefer still or slow moving streams or lakes and they cannot survive in cold water. They form large groups mainly for defense rather than to hunt.

Feeding Pattern

Piranhas are omnivorous, and can be both scavengers and predators. They mainly eat fish, plants, and insects, but they will also feed on dead animals or attack live ones that have fallen into the water. When water levels are high your risk of being attacked is virtually nil, but during the dry season,

when food is scarce, they will become desperate and take whatever they can get. During low water season they are themselves
more vulnerable to attack from predators such as dolphins and
caimans (a type of crocodilian reptile), so piranhas are more
aggressive at these times.

Piranhas are day feeders and they rest at night, so that is
the best time to avoid them. Although, you are at greater risk
of being attacked by other night-feeding predators such as
caimans. However, caimans tend to stop feeding as conditions
become dryer.

Blood Detectors

Piranhas can detect blood and are attracted to the tini-
est bit of it in the water, so stay out of the water if you have
any open cuts or if you are menstruating. If you have recently
handled raw meat (e.g. have been gutting fish), this will also
attract unwanted attention.

Good Vibrations

Try to disturb the water as little as possible, and don't
make any noise. Piranhas are sensitive to the finest vibrations, and if you thrash around and splash the piranhas will be
alerted to your presence and may strike. Human attacks are most
common in places where lots of people bathe at the same time.

131. Go Whoring in Tangier

If swearing, cursing, drinking, and whoring are your thing, head over to Tangier, a legendary town on the coast of northern Morocco, and one of the oldest in North Africa. William Burroughs hung out here with Jack Kerouac and other beat writers, and everyone else from Truman Capote to Henry Matisse has enjoyed its hospitality. Mark Twain endorsed it at the end of *The Innocents Abroad*: "I would seriously recommend to the Government of the United States that when a man commits a crime so heinous that the law provides no adequate punishment for it, they make him Consul-General to Tangier."

Whore Guides

The scene in Tangier isn't as outrageous as it was in its heyday in the 1950s, but there is still plenty of debauchery. As soon as you leave the airport, train station, or ferry, you will be inundated with locals offering to be your tour guide. If you are feeling reckless, ask one of them to take you to the nearest brothel. If you don't want their help, say, *"laa, shukran"* ("no, thanks" in Arabic) and stride away purposefully.

Nightlife

The nightlife in Tangier is quite depressing, but go into any bar or one of the many nightclubs and just about every Moroccan woman is a prostitute (even the ones who just look like prostitutes). The music is not at all like you'd hear in a club back home: this is classical Arabic music, improvized around various melody lines, and sounds like a cross between symphonic and Indian string music.

If you want gay sex, most of the tourist guides will try to procure you prostitutes of both sexes, so you won't be short on offers. Men and women will also approach you in restaurants (even good ones) and offer their services.

Stay Sober

Don't get too drunk, as you'll need to keep your wits about you to avoid being ripped off or robbed, and drunkenness is frowned upon in this Muslim country (many establishments don't offer alcohol).

Haggle

Be prepared to negotiate. When buying a carpet in Tangier you can usually haggle the price down to an eighth of the asking price. It's the same with personal services. Be sure to practice safe sex; Tangier has the one of the highest rates of HIV-positive sex workers in the world.

132. Drive Your Neighbor Away

Eric Hoffer said, "It is easier to love humanity as a whole than to love one's neighbor." Fortunately, it's real easy to make your neighbor's life a living hell.

1. **Paint cuss words on his immaculate front lawn using weed killer. In a few days, the grass will turn brown and die, and your profanities will magically appear.**

2. Staying on the weed killer theme, sneak into your neighbor's backyard and paint a circle about six feet in diameter. A few days later when the grass has died, stick a stake in the middle of the circle, then shave bald patches on their dog and tie it on a short leash to the stake. Call animal welfare.

3. Put up a sign outside their house saying "ALL BROKEN FRIDGES GRATEFULLY RECEIVED," or have a garage sale to sell off their stuff while they are away on vacation.

4. Find out where your neighbor shops and buy exactly the same outfits. Always wear them one day after your neighbor does.

5. Every time you see your neighbor washing his car, gardening, cleaning out his garage, etc., say "How would you like to do mine when you're finished?"

6. Keep yelling at imaginary kids to "Be quiet! You'll disturb the neighbors."

7. Begin a fifteen-year construction project on your house.

8. Float unwrapped chocolate bars and toilet paper in your neighbor's pool.

9. Make him think his car has an oil leak by pouring a little oil under the engine every morning.

10. Block his drains with human remains.

133. Pick Someone's Pocket

The great benefit of pick-pocketing is that you can earn thousands in a few hours without the need to mug people at gun point. Also, some of your victims won't even know they've been robbed, and they will blame themselves for leaving their purse in a shop. If you are thinking of pressing up against a few people in the subway, here are some pick-pocketing tips to get you started.

Dress Against Type

What's your mental picture of a pickpocket? He is probably a scrawny male scumbag between the ages of sixteen and thirty. But this picture is wrong. Many pickpockets dress to resemble the type of people you would least expect to rob you: wealthy businessmen, tourists, and middle-class mothers with babies.

Opportunism

Often it doesn't take much skill to steal a purse or mobile phone. Go to any crowded public area and you'll see people sitting around with their bags unattended. A guy who sticks his wallet in the back pocket of his pants or in the outside pocket of his loose-fitting coat is practically asking for it. Carry a jacket or newspaper to cover your hands while you work.

– Distraction   –

Your greatest weapon is distraction. Pickpockets often work in groups, so that while one or more members of the gang cause a distraction, the other one lifts the victim's belongings. Here are some common distraction techniques:

1. Have a fight with one of your accomplices, while the other members of your gang steal the belongings of those who gather to watch.

2. One of you accidentally drops the contents of your handbag all over the floor. When a kind person squats down to help pick things up, another gets busy in her pockets.

3. Go to any place where there is a ready-made distraction, such as street theater. The crowd there is easy pickings.

4. The "stall" stops suddenly in front of your victim, so that another member of your gang (the "pick") bumps into them, and steals their wallet, while making a big deal of apologizing. The mark will not suspect the pick because their attention (and possible irritation and frustration) is focused on the stall.

Follow the Money

Announce to your friend in a loud voice "Someone stole my wallet!" The reaction of those around you will be to pat their own wallets to make sure they are still there. Perfect. Now you know where they keep their valuables. Also, watch people at the ATMs and shop checkouts to see where they put their wallets and purses when they leave. Also, you can brush past them to feel for the bulge their wallet makes (this is called "fanning").

134. Sober Up Quickly

Unfortunately there is no quick way to sober up—not cold showers, fresh air, or black coffee. Alcohol will stay in your body until it is broken down by your liver and eventually leaves your body through breath, sweat, and urine.

How Does Alcohol Work?

When you drink alcohol, it enters the bloodstream through your stomach and intestines. Then the bloodstream carries it to other parts of the body and it reaches the brain almost immediately. Alcohol is a depressant so it gets to work immediately inhibiting brain function.

Time is the only thing that can sober you up. Your liver needs time to break down the alcohol. The body can metabolize half an ounce of ethanol per hour. A standard drink contains just under half an ounce of ethanol, so you must allow about one hour for every standard drink you consume.

That said, there are a few things you can do to create the illusion of sobriety:

Eating Food Slows Down Alcohol Absorption

Food slows the absorption of alcohol into the bloodstream (but eventually the alcohol will be absorbed and impairment will occur). Nevertheless, if you've just had a few drinks, eat some fatty food and your body will absorb the alcohol more slowly. In effect, this is the reverse of sobering up, since the alcohol stays in your body longer, but you will stand more chance of seeing the evening out.

Drink Regularly to Increase Your Tolerance

Hardened drinkers increase their tolerance to alcohol. Several years of regular drinking actually trains your liver to break down alcohol more efficiently, with the added bonus that your brain cells become less sensitive to its effects. This won't affect your blood alcohol concentration (so you will still fail a Breathalyzer if you're over the limit), but it will make you feel less drunk.

Drink Lots of Water

Drink lots of water to help your liver get rid of the alcohol. It also reduces the chances of you getting a hangover, which is most often caused by dehydration and vitamin deficiencies.

135. Travel to Volatile Countries

Back by popular demand, here are another five dangerous destinations that you'd be an idiot to head to. There still isn't room for Burundi, Sri Lanka, and the Gaza Strip, but in no particular order, avoid these first:

Pakistan

Here, westerners are the target of suicide bombings from extremist Islamic groups, which have spread beyond their tribal bases and are trying to take over the entire nuclear-armed nation. The tribal areas bordering Afghanistan are especially volatile.

Haiti

Violence and political instability are the norm; police corruption is widespread and the country has descended into lawlessness. Outside of the tourist resorts, visitors are at great risk of being robbed, raped, kidnapped, or murdered.

Liberia

In 2003 the civil war ended, but the fragile peace is still being policed by a U.N. peacekeeping force, and crime is a major threat, including theft, rape, and murder.

Chad

The country is very unstable with much fighting between various ethnic groups, especially at the border with the Darfur region of Sudan. Many westerners have been robbed at checkpoints and on the roads.

Sudan

The United States has listed Sudan as a state sponsor of terrorism since 1993. The western region of Darfur is the most dangerous area of the country, as government-backed Janjaweed militias continue to terrorize locals in the name of suppressing anti-government rebels.

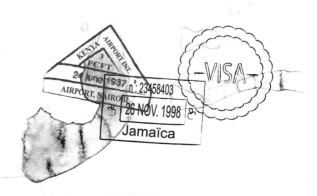

136. Find a Hidden Tribe in the Amazon

There are thought to be about 100 hidden tribes in the world, of which more than half are in the Brazilian and Peruvian Amazon. The best place to search for lost tribes is Brazil, where there are thought to be about forty, with another fifteen in Peru and a smattering in Bolivia, Paraguay, Ecuador, and Colombia. In other parts of the world, the lost tribes are in western Papua, parts of Indonesia, and North Sentinel Island in the Indian Ocean.

Very little is known about their society and technology, or the extent of their territory. However, they are presently under threat from logging and oil exploration, and the history of contact between indigenous tribes and the outside world has been unfavorable, if you do track down a tribe, don't expect a warm welcome. Isolated tribes are understandably willing to kill intruders to protect their lands.

1. To reach a hidden tribe you will probably have to spend two weeks traveling on the river, followed by three weeks of continual bushwhacking through dense tropical jungle—the most hostile environment in the world after the Poles.

2. Don't grab vines with your bare hands because many of them have thorns and can lacerate your palms; despite what you have seen in Tarzan movies, you can't always break open a vine and drink the water inside the stem. If the water is red, yellow, or milky, have a Diet Pepsi instead.

3. Remember, many species of poisonous snakes are remarkably small, and your biggest threats are from tiny insects, or infected cuts and bites.

4. Drink plenty of water, but go to the bathroom before you go to sleep, as the chance of getting bitten by malaria infected mosquitoes is exponentially proportional to the number of times you have to pee during the night.

5. If you see a freshly hacked sapling, dangling by a piece of bark lying across your path, this is a warning to stay away.

6. If you develop any form of sickness, even the common cold, turn back. These tribes have no resistance to even the everyday viruses that are an inconvenience for us, but a possible death sentence for them.

137. Tell if Your Neighbor Is a Zombie

Nothing brings down property prices in your area quicker than the discovery that you have a reanimated human corpse living next door. Your neighbor seems never to sleep, his lack of free will is alarming to say the least, and his craving for human flesh means you live in constant fear for your life. However, before you run over there with a chain saw, spend a little time observing his movements to make sure that he really is a member of the undead, rather than a Goth or Keith Richards.

What Is a Zombie?

First decide which of the two types of zombie that you are dealing with: Hollywood B-movie zombie or Haitian voodoo zombie. The former is a human corpse that has come back to "life," while the latter has had his free will and "Ti Bon Ange"

(Creole for "little good angel") or soul removed by a sorcerer. To keep things simple, let's assume that you are most likely to be troubled by the Hollywood B-movie strain.

Characteristics

Zombies enjoy groaning and milling around in groups. Personal hygiene is poor: for example, your neighbor might have an arm hanging off, wear tattered clothing, and reek of rotting flesh. Other tell-tale signs include:

If he could understand the question, "Where do you see yourself in five years time?", he would probably answer "Still feasting on the brains of the living." All other hobbies and interests will have been subsumed by his all-consuming and unquenchable hunger for fresh human flesh

Unresponsive to communication

Pale complexion and clammy skin

Anything less subtle than a baseball bat is unlikely to discourage him from invading your personal space or biting your neck

Dull expression of the eyes

Lumbering gait, often with hands held out in front of the body at arms length

Insensible to pain (for example, he doesn't cry out when you step on his foot, cut off his arm, or try to run him over repeatedly with your car)

How to Destroy Your Zombie Neighbor

If you can't run away or he corners you in an alley with a bunch of his friends, you should either burn or decapitate him. Zombies are highly susceptible to fire or electrocution. It is a common misconception that they have superhuman strength. In fact, their poor agility and coordination make them an easy target for your average flame thrower and/or M79 grenade launcher.

138. Break Into a Car

There are two groups of people who break into cars. In the first group are career criminals who spray paint the car, remove the engine block security numbers, change the plates, and sell it. People in this group already know how to break into cars. So if you're reading this, you must be part of the second group: you're a twelve-year-old joyriding punk who didn't get enough attention when you were little. Hi kid. Did you steal this book too?

Here's what you do:

1. Only break into a car with an automatic transmission, since you probably can't drive a manual. The downside is that an automatic is more likely to have a car alarm.

2. Any car with a flashing light on or near the dash has a car alarm, so move on. Any car with a light on top of the roof is a cop car. You definitely don't want to steal that.

3. You can learn a lot about the driver by looking at the seat. If it is set low and pulled back with a big butt-sized indent in it, you know the car is driven by a 250-pound steroid-popping freak who will rip your arms off if he catches you. Choose a car with the seat forward and high—it's probably driven by a woman.

4. If you just want to joyride rather than sell the car, hammer a large flathead screwdriver in the keyhole and turn hard (this should break the pins and allow you to turn the chamber). Or use a lock-out tool kit.

5. Bring a cushion with you; even when you've raised the seat as far as it will go, you'll still need it to help you see over the steering wheel.

6. To start the car, if you've got a manufacturer's key, use that, otherwise on older models you can splice the two red wires underneath or inside the dash, or stick a screw hammer into the ignition and pop it out, then use a screwdriver to turn the brass triangle.

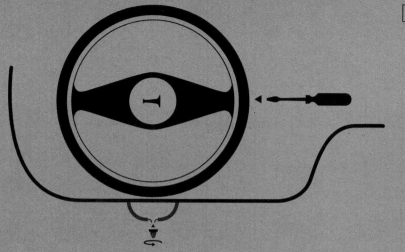

7. Use your seatbelt. That way, when the cops start chasing you and you wrap the car around a tree, you'll walk away with your life. You've got a bright future ahead of you. In five years, you should be clearing $3,000 a week dealing drugs, so don't mess it up by getting wasted too early.

139. Shoplift

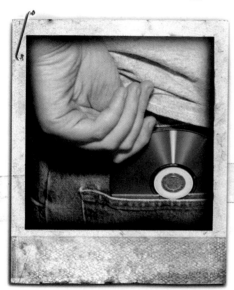

You don't need us to tell you that shoplifting is a criminal act, but we should also draw your attention to the morality of screwing over the big boys like Walmart and Target versus hitting the small independent shops. That's a matter for your own conscience.

Recon Mission

It's a good idea to check out a store before you actually steal anything from it. This allows you to locate the surveillance cameras and to work out where the blind spots are. On this visit, buy a couple of small inexpensive items so you look like a regular shopper. Beware of mirrors on the walls at corners as they usually have cameras in them. Check out the obesity of the security guard. Ideally, he should be morbidly obese and incapable of chasing you without popping an artery. Beware the little scrawny guards; not only are they quick on their feet, but they also have more to prove.

Go Solo

Nothing is more suspicious than a group of three or four shoplifters, especially if they are teenagers. Go alone but make sure you've got a getaway driver outside with the engine running. Walk into the store casually and greet the door greeter. His or her job is to make you feel welcome, but also to make potential shoplifters feel noticed, because thieves thrive on anonymity. But you're a regular shopper, right, so don't let this phase you. Remember the odds are in your favor: in the U.S., as many as one in twelve customers is a shoplifter, and each one commits an average of fifty thefts before being caught.

Have a Purpose

If you walk into a shop with the sole aim of stealing something, it will show. So you need to buy a few specific (but cheap) items, so that you don't raise suspicion by wandering aimlessly around the store. Always have enough money in your wallet to pay for the stolen items as well, so that if you get caught you can burst into tears and say it was a one-time thing and offer to pay (tell them your mother just died and this is your way of grieving). Pick up your target item, along with some of your smaller things, then walk to a camera blind spot, pocket it, and then take something from the shelf to show you have an innocent reason for being there.

Trust Your Instinct

If at any time you get a bad feeling, trust your instinct. Accept that today is an off day and put the stuff back. Walk out of the shop. Even if you get stopped, you can't be arrested if you haven't taken stuff off the premises. If you have stolen something and the alarm sounds at the exit, keep walking. They can only stop and search you if they have actually seen you steal. They can't lay a finger on you otherwise, so keep walking and threaten legal action if anyone tries to detain you, because they aren't cops.

140. Have a Kidney Transplant in the Philippines

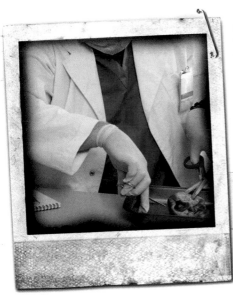

During the last decade, the Philippines was transplant tourists's number one destination (other hot spots include China, Pakistan, Egypt, and Colombia), and as many as 500 wealthy foreigners visited the country to buy a kidney cheaply from an impoverished citizen.

Government Crackdown

In 2008, the government changed the law on the sale of organs, and it is now illegal for foreigners to have transplant surgery in the country, unless they are related to Filipino citizens by blood. The Philippines still remains one of the world's cheapest places for wealthy foreign patients wanting to buy a new kidney though, but now if you get caught you face up to twenty years in prison and a fine of up to 2 million pesos (approximately $45,000).

— One Kidney Island —

Procure the organ through one of the many brokers who trawls the slums of Manila and the provinces looking for potential donors. One area of Manila has earned the nickname "One Kidney Island" because so many of its inhabitants have sold a kidney. The brokers charge up to $1,500 per transplant and often put up the donors in safe houses or hotels for months until a suitable recipient can be found.

The way it used to work was that you could buy an organ and then the hospital would classify the transaction as a donation. You paid the hospital about $50,000 while a kidney cost you between $2,000 and $10,000 (an enormous sum for a poor family). The hospitals were only supposed to allow ten percent of their transplant patients to be foreigners, but in practice nearly 60 percent of hospitals were exceeding their quota and breaking Health Department guidelines.

Today, you can still have the surgery, but kidney donations are now monitored by a new regulatory body, so you will either have to pay large bribes, or have underground surgery, which brings a higher risk of complications.

141. Track Down the Most Poisonous Animals

When normal people go on safari they want to see the Big Five: lion, leopard, elephant, rhinoceros, and African buffalo. But where's the danger in that? An intrepid traveler like you should use the following checklist when planning your wild safari. Here's a list of the world's most poisonous animals— much cooler than the Big Five. Don't get too close though; you might be heading home in the cargo hold.

Poison Dart Frog

It has *poison* in its *name*. This brightly colored little creature is definitely no Kermit. However, one touch and you'll certainly be feeling green. In order to see one in the wild, you'll need to travel to the rainforests of Central and South America. Ones in captivity do not secret poison (at least not much) since the toxic chemical emission is actually a build up of the poisonous chemicals from their prey.

Deathstalker Scorpion

To find this dangerous creature, head to the deserts of North Africa or the Middle East. Besides being yellow and relatively lightly armored, it's not a typical scorpion species as its sting is very poisonous and very painful. If stung, the neurotoxins it releases will cause an intense pain followed by an agonizing fever before you finally slip into a coma.

Blue-ringed Octopus

You will need to go underwater to find this member of the Poisonous Five. And being about the size of a ping-pong ball with the ability to camouflage itself (the vibrant blue rings on its skin aren't visible unless provoked), it is going to be a hard one to locate. Be very cautious as you check the coral and rock crevices for this tiny wonder. There is no known antidote for the poison contained in the animal's saliva. One bite and you better hope you're near a respirator because you will need assistance breathing until the toxins work out of your system, which usually takes about twenty-four hours. If you're still up for the challenge, its habitat is shallow Pacific tide pools, anywhere from Australia to Japan.

Inland Taipan

All this snake wants is to be left alone. Unfortunately, as the world's most poisonous land snake, it has found its way on to the list. Found in the heart of Australia, its scales change color depending on the season so you will need to be mindful of what month it is before you go searching for this serpent. If it is winter, you should be on the lookout for the dark brown scales. If it is summer, you want to watch for a snake that is more of an olive-green. The bite from an inland taipan contains enough venom to kill 100 humans, but as mentioned, it is a rather docile creature. So look; don't poke it with a stick.

Sydney Funnel-web Spider

Stay Down Under to catch a glimpse of the last of the Poisonous Five. The Sydney funnel-web spider is native to—you guessed it—Sydney, Australia. Only males contain the venom component that is dangerous to your nervous system. But they are also the ones who leave the burrow in order to find a mate, and can sometimes wander into homes. They can get up to about three inches and length and typically have a glossy bluish-black to dark plum color. If you do end up spotting one, stay away. This species of arachnid is quite aggressive and will attack.

142. Break 200 MPH on the Autobahn

There are few places on the planet where you can drive a passenger car as fast as you want; the German Autobahn is one of them. However, there are only a handful of production cars in the world capable of breaking the magic 200 mph barrier.

Buy Some Wheels

You need to spend a minimum of $120,000 to buy a car that will break 200 mph, and then more like $150,000 if you want something classy like a Porsche Carrera Turbo. A cheaper alternative would be to spend about $50,000 on the car and hundreds of hours (and dollars) in the workshop to adapt something like a Corvette.

There's a world of difference between doing 180 and 200 because the wind resistance increases exponentially, and you need a third more power to gain ten percent more speed. The first production car that could exceed 200 mph was the Ferrari F40, launched in 1987. Next came RUF's 469 bhp CTR "Yellowbird," and then the McLaren F1 hit 242 mph in 1993, which no one could beat for a decade. Now we are entering another golden age with speeds heading towards 300 mph in the next few years. Today, a

Bugatti Veyron will comfortably reach 250 mph and still feel very stable, but it well set you back well over a million dollars.

Hit the Road

Before your attempt, familiarize yourself with a flat, dry stretch of Autobahn because even the slightest curve can become a challenge when you're speeding. Also, travel in the early morning, mid-morning, or at night when the roads are quietest. Get someone else to check the speedometer because if you take your eye off the road for a second you will travel blindly 293 feet (you travel a mile every 18 seconds). If someone a quarter of a mile away pulled out into your lane doing 50 mph, you'd hit them in less than six seconds if you didn't ease off the gas and apply the brake.

More than half of the German Autobahn has no speed restrictions, so you've got about 6,835 miles to play around with. The Autobahn is actually safer than U.S. highways because drivers have to be 18 before they can get behind the wheel, the testing is more rigorous, the left lane is only used for passing, the road surface is better quality, and, let's be honest, Germans drive better and safer cars.

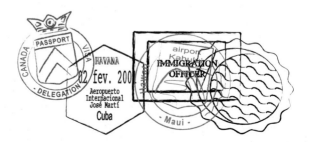

143. Travel to the Future

Time traveling into the future is easier than traveling into the past. Dystopian writers have predicted the horrors that await us there, but the future can't be that bad because it hasn't happened yet; paradoxically, this is precisely the reason why it's theoretically possible to go there.

Models of Future Time Travel

There are two models of future time travel. In one model, you leave your present and travel to a future in which you are only present as the future traveler, since you have removed yourself from the present (and hence the future) at your moment of travel. In other words, if you had a driving test tomorrow and you wanted to see if you passed or failed, you would travel in time to tomorrow, where you would discover that you hadn't taken the test at all, since you had inexplicably gone missing.

In the second model, you are transported to your own personal future, where you may even meet your future self (so long as you don't travel beyond your own natural lifetime). You could even shake hands with yourself on your deathbed.

POLICE NA
Aéroport de
26 NOV. 1
FRANCE

Methods of Future Time Travel

Physics allows for future time travel without building a fictional "time machine." Simply travel away from the earth at close that the speed of light for a few years, then turn around and travel back home. Einstein showed that time is relative to the observer, so you will find that scores of years have passed on Earth and everyone you ever knew will be dead. Alternatively, take up temporary residence inside a hollow high-mass object, or just outside the event horizon of a black hole.

Three Things That Shouldn't Happen in the Future

1. If life is a computer-generated illusion and human beings are nothing more than wet cells that generate electricity for their mechanical overlords, and you manage to stop four sentinels just by thinking it, don't let anyone reason that you could pull it off with a sloppy answer like: "Because you are the One."

2. If Kevin Costner's *Waterworld* is the reality and drinking-water has become one of the world's rarest commodities, explain to the raft-dwellers of the future that they can desalinate sea water by simply boiling it and then collecting the condensation.

3. If you've been to the year 3000, where not much has changed but they live underwater, you will NOT encounter the great-great-great-granddaughter of anyone from your own time—she would have died during the 23rd century.

144. Hang, Draw, and Quarter

It was the British who introduced the torture of hang,
draw, and quarter as punishment for the crime of treason. It was first used by King
Edward I in 1283 on the Welsh
prince Dafydd ap Gruffydd. It
was thought to be the cruelest
form of capital punishment and
was only used on men.

1. Make sure that the felon
is male. If the subject is
shown to be a female, she
should not suffer to be hanged,
drawn, and quartered, but
should instead be burned at the
stake. This method should only
be used for high treason. Petty treason is punishable by mere
hanging without dismemberment.

2. Tie the criminal to a wooden frame and drag him through
the streets to the place of execution. This allows the
townsfolk to verbally and physically abuse him, each according
to their own desires.

3. First, make a noose and hang the felon by his neck.

4. If the felon has paid you handsomely, make sure he is dead
before proceeding to the next stage—the "drawing."

5. If the felon has failed to bribe you, cut open his abdomen so that his innards fall onto the floor while he is still alive.

6. Hold the entrails up and display them to the assembled crowd.

7. Cut off the genitalia and burn these together with the viscera in plain view of the dying victim.

8. After he is dead, take him from the scaffold, behead the corpse, and cut the body into four pieces—this is called "quartering."

9. Display each of the five body parts (the four quarters and the head) in different prominent positions around town as a deterrent to other would-be traitors— this is called "gibbeting."

145. Place a Gypsy Curse

Can you rokra Romany?
Can you play the bosh?
Can you jal adrey the staripen?
Can you chin the cost?

Can you speak the Roman tongue?
Can you play the fiddle?
Can you eat the prison-loaf?
Can you cut and whittle?

A gypsy curse can either be an insult or the effective action of some power, distinguished solely by the quality of adversity that it brings. Three conditions have to be met in order for your gypsy curse to work.

1. You must believe that the person you are cursing has transgressed an acceptable code of conduct. You can't curse someone if they've done nothing wrong.

2. The person you have cursed must be made aware that they have been cursed.

3. They must also believe that you have the power and responsibility to lay a curse on them.

Here are some choice gypsy curses to get you started, but it is more effective to invent your own:

1. "May you wander over the face of the earth forever, never sleep twice in the same bed, never drink water twice from the same well, and never cross the same river twice in a year" (this is probably the most famous gypsy curse in the world).

2. "May your daughter's hair grow thick and abundant, all over her face."

3. "May the IRS disallow all your deductions."

4. "May the fleas of a thousand dead camels infest one of your errogenous zones."

5. "May your every wish be granted."

6. "May your left ear wither and fall into your right pocket."

7. "May you get slightly fatter every year."

146. Streak at a Sporting Event

Streaking is usually defined as "the non-sexual act of taking off one's clothes and running naked through a public place." Therefore it is important while you are cavorting around naked that you don't do anything that can be interpreted as overtly sexual, such as taking yourself in hand, sitting on the umpire's face, or getting an erection. Streaking should be harmless fun. Sure you'll get arrested and heavily fined, but that shouldn't stop you from relishing your five minutes of fame. Above all, remember to smile.

Crowd Pleaser

Remember you are primarily streaking for your own enjoyment and to show off to your friends. If the crowd is with you, then that's a bonus. The reception you receive from the crowd is dependent upon whether you are male or female. Male streakers are usually treated with contempt by the players, but for some reason the sight of a nice pair of funbags generates considerably less hostility.

Can I Afford It?

Be aware that in recent years broadcasters have been discouraged from filming streakers, so it is unlikely that you will appear on TV, as the camera will cut away the moment you appear. However, the fine for streaking has increased considerably, so you might want to consider copying Lisa Lewis, who sold her bikini on trademe.com after streaking at the Waikato Stadium in 2006 during a rugby match between the All Blacks and Ireland.

Pick Your Moment

Leave at least half an hour between eating a large meal and streaking, as the crowd wants to see the bouncing beauty of the human body, not the contents of your stomach.

Time your streak so that it doesn't interfere with direct play, for example, while the field goal kicker is lining up for an extra point, or while a soccer player is taking a free kick. Never strip when the Pakistan cricket team is playing Ireland. It takes a lot of concentration to deliberately lose a match and your unwelcome appearance could easily throw them back on their game; the last thing you want is to get on the wrong side of criminal gambling syndicates.

While streaking and certain sports just don't go together (NASCAR racing, global yacht racing, and bobsledding spring to mind), don't feel you have to restrict yourself to streaking at baseball and football games. In January 2000, twenty-two-year-old waitress Tracy Seargant ran naked down the green of the Indoor Bowls Championship.

147. Ward Off Evil Spirits

There are many ancient ways of warding off evil spirits and protecting yourself from the evil eye.

1. Make extensive use of gargoyles as a design feature on your house. Their ugly faces and grotesque expressions scare away evil spirits.

2. Use an amulet to provide protection against harm. It can be worn around the neck or kept in your pocket, and it can take many forms including protective hands, fish, angels, diamonds, written charms, human finger bones, tiger's teeth, rabbit's feet, goat's feet, Egyptian scarab, arrowheads, knuckle bones from a piece of mutton, pine cones, and toads.

3. The use of certain plants and herbs is effective, such as agrimony, anise seed, aloe, angelica, basil, caraway seeds, fennel, garlic, hazel, majoram, willow (good for magic wands), vervain, and wintergreen. Scatter tea leaves in front of your house.

4. Bless someone when they sneeze.

5. When you spill salt, throw a pinch of it over your left shoulder (that's the side of your body where evil spirits dwell).

6. A yawn is a sign that Death is summoning you, so cover your mouth when you yawn or evil spirits will enter your body through it.

7. Tying knots in your handkerchief helps you to remember something because a knot is a charm against evil.

8. When baking, remember to mark your loaves with a cross.

9. Mummify a cat and brick it up in the wall of your house.

10. Hang a horseshoe above the door. Evil spirits linger in doorways. That's why a bride must be carried over the threshold.

11. Drip wax from a Paschal Candle between the horns of your livestock to protect them from disease caused by evil elves and witches.

12. Kill any hen that persistently crows before it destroys its eggs and teaches other hens to do likewise. It has the Devil inside it.

13. Whenever you ahear the hoot of an owl, put irons in your fire, or throw salt or vinegar into the fire; or remove your clothes, turn them inside out, and put them back on.

14. Ring bells and bang pots and pans after a wedding ceremony. The bridesmaids dress up finely to act as decoy brides and confuse evil spirits.

15. On Friday the 13th, walk around your house thirteen times.

148. Build Freakish Muscles

Irrespective of age and gender, every physique has the capacity to build big muscle, provided it is trained and given rest at proper periods. There are countless build-rock-hard-muscle formulas on the Internet, promising guaranteed satisfaction or your money back, accompanied by pictures of guys who have added thirty pounds of muscle in just twelve weeks. Ignore them. Here are some genuine muscle-building tips to help you get awesome and ripped.

1. Allow your body adequate time to recuperate between training sessions. One of the pitfalls of "hard gainers" (those who build muscle slowly) is overtraining. Go to the gym for an hour, three to four times a week. Never go two days in a row. This allows your body time to rest, keeps you from getting bored, and enables you to be more focused when you are working out.

2. Perform low reps with high weights, but remember that good form is more important than the amount of weight you are lifting. You can only target muscle if you can control the weight. If your dumbbell curls look like jerks, you've got bad style. Lower the weight and stop trying to impress other gym users.

3. Use free weights instead of machine and cable exercises.

4. Surprise your muscles and keep your training fresh by varying the exercises, the number of reps, the tempo of the reps; and by gradually increasing the weight every couple of weeks. You've got to mix things up to make maximum gains. Train to total muscle failure on at least a few sets every workout.

5. Don't waste time training your abs to get a six pack. Fat is burned all over the body when you train, not just in certain areas. Lose weight and your six pack will appear.

6. Eat at least two grams of protein per pound of body weight. If you weigh 150 pounds, you need to eat at least 300 grams of protein. Eat a small meal every two to three hours.

7. Drink at least eight glasses of water a day and get at least eight hours of sleep each night.

8. Inject yourself daily with HGH (Human Growth Hormone), a 191-amino acid, single chain polypeptide that occurs naturally in the human body and is produced by the pituitary gland. What's the worst that can happen? Your bones growing out of shape and heart disease? A small price to pay for freakish muscle growth.

149. Hitchhike from LA to NYC

Just how crazy, optimistic, or suicidal do you have to be to hitchhike today? Hello—are you living in the '80s? Actually, it's not all that bad—if you know what you're doing. However, if just waiting for a bus makes you bored, then hitching will likely kill you.

1. Before you start, buy some maps, so you can figure out which rides are actually taking you closer to your destination rather than to some crazy trucker's lock-up.

2. Wear bright clean clothing so that drivers can see you, but not so bright that drivers think that you are a nutcase (or French).

3. Don't hitch from the center of town; get a bus to the edge of town.

4. Choose a hitching spot where you can be seen clearly from a long way off, and where drivers can stop safely and legally. Hitching on the highway is illegal, but you'll have to weigh the benefit of traffic flow versus getting arrested.

5. It's safer to travel with a companion, but being part of a trio won't get you very far at all. You'll get picked up mostly by solitary male drivers in empty cars, and some females. Also, try to avoid squeezing into a full car where you're outnumbered.

6. If you have waited an hour, start walking in the direction you want to go. Sometimes it's even better to accept a short ride in the wrong direction to a better pick-up point than wait in a bad place. Be prepared to do a lot of walking and stay cheerful. If you treat a lift as a bonus, you'll have a better mental attitude.

7. Pack plenty of food and water, as you never know where your next rest stop will be—and gas stations are expensive.

8. Don't give the driver your final destination; this leaves you an excuse to be dropped off if you feel uncomfortable.

9. A highway rest area is a good place to ask around for a lift while people are refuelling their cars. It avoids the illegality of hitching on the highway itself. Expect plenty of rejections, but it does give both parties more of a chance to size each other up. However, many hitchhikers avoid rest areas because there's a greater risk of being picked up by a serial mugger or rapist. The more commercial rest areas on toll roads are probably your safest option.

150. Join the Mile High Club

The MHC is always open to new members. There is no dress code, membership fee, or stuffy protocol; in fact, the only entry requirement is engaging in sexual intercourse on board an airplane while it is in flight, at least 1 mile (5,280 feet) above the ground.

Founding Members

The founders of the MHC are thought to be the pilot Lawrence Sperry and Mrs. Waldo Polk, while on board a Curtiss Flying Boat en route to New York in November 1916. Sperry engaged the auto pilot which he designed himself, and got to work with the married woman.

Legal Implications

You can be arrested for public indecency if your coupling takes place in view of other passengers. If you get it on in the toilet or in one of the double beds in the new Airbus A380, then the legality depends on the airline you are flying with, your departure and destination points, and which country you were over flying at the time.

In 1999, two married strangers in business class on an American Airlines flight from Dallas to Manchester were arrested for performing sex acts in view of other passengers. After downing two bottles of wine and several glasses of cognac and port, the woman stripped to her underwear halfway through the in-flight movie when the lights were dimmed and the couple refused to stop despite repeated requests from the flight crew, even after the lights had been switched on. They were arrested by Manchester police upon landing and both lost their jobs. At the time, the woman worked for Nortel Networks, whose TV advertising slogan was "come together." Sometimes you can be too on-message.

Celebrity Mile-highers

Virgin Atlantic Airways owner Richard Branson claims to have joined the MHC when he was 19 by having sex with a married woman in the toilet (he didn't know she was married at the time). Ralph Fiennes is alleged to have had sex with flight attendant Lisa Roberston in a business class lavatory on board a Qantas flight bound for Mumbai in February 2007. She lost her job and Fiennes has made no comment.

Charter a Flight

Part of the thrill of having sex in the air, apart from the heightened sensations many report due to the reduced air pressure, is the illicit nature of the act, and the chance of getting caught. However, several companies offer private charter flights for the risk-averse who want to get it on in the air.

151. Become a Cliff-Diving Thrill Seeker

Cliff diving or "tombstoning" leaves little room for error. When you jump from a height of eighty feet, your body is subjected to ten Gs and the impact as you hit the water is the equivalent of slamming into concrete from a height of twenty feet, so your entry has to be correct or you're in serious trouble.

Here are the top six places to get your cliff diving on:

1. Kahekili's Leap, Lanai, Hawaii

This is the birthplace of cliff diving. Kahekili was an eighteenth-century king who instructed his Nakoa warriors to display their bravery and loyalty by freefalling seventy feet over jagged rocks into the clear blue ocean below. The practice was called *lele kawa*.

2. Wolfgangsee, Austria

Each summer the cliffs at Hochzeitskreuz, Wolfgangsee play host to the Red Bull Cliff Diving World Championships where the fourteen best cliff divers in the world jump from a height of eighty-eight feet in front of three thousand fans. They somersault and twist in the air for 2.5 seconds before hitting the water at fifty-five miles per hour.

3. La Quebrada, Acapulco, Mexico

The spot's name means "The Break" in Spanish, and this is one of the top tourist attractions in Mexico. The cliff jump is sixty feet high. Divers must time their jump precisely because the water level changes as the waves roll in and out of the cove. Formed in 1934, La Quebrada Cliff Divers still perform death-defying cliff jumps nightly while holding torches.

4. Ponte Brolla, Vallemaggia, Switzerland

The World High Diving Federation Cliff Diving European Championships is held here regularly, but there is a range of diving heights from junior (thirty feet) to more challenging (sixty-five feet). If splitting your head or feet open on impact isn't painful enough, the icy water will probably give you a heart attack.

5. Porto Venere, Italy

Porto Venere is a beautiful medieval town on the Ligurian coast of Italy, south of the Cinque Terre known worldwide for its natural beauty. There are lots of cliff-diving venues on this coast, but this is one of the best.

6. Red Rocks Park, South Burlington, Vermont

Vermont is loaded with good cliff diving, but Red Rocks Park offers drops of up to seventy-six feet, with narrow rock walls to increase the chances of fatal injury. Jumping into the icy waters here requires even greater precision than other dive sites.